CAT
KNITS

CAT KNITS

Melinda Coss

AURUM PRESS

ACKNOWLEDGEMENTS

To Gingypop, Sparky, Geraldine
Berkowitz, Priscilla and Loney, without
whom this book would not have
been possible.
   I should like to thank Robert Mackintosh
for his photography, Justine, Hilary and
Les for their modelling, Sue Neville for
knitting through the night, and The Really
Useful Theatre Company for allowing
the inclusion of cats from their
wonderful show.

Copyright © Melinda Coss 1988

First published 1988 by Aurum Press Limited
33 Museum Street, London WC1A 1LD

Produced by the Justin Knowles Publishing Group
9 Colleton Crescent, Exeter EX2 4BY

ISBN 0 948149 93 0

Printed and bound in Italy by New Interlitho

CONTENTS

INTRODUCTION

If you are lucky enough to be owned by a cat, you may like to create his or her own personalized cushion or jumper and, provided you fit the image into the appropriate graph size for your selected jumper, this task will not be too difficult. You will need a good clear photograph to fit the appropriate graph. If the size of your photograph is too small or too large to fit, it is possible to have it enlarged or reduced at a photocopy shop for 10p or so. (If you do not have a photocopy shop in your area, send your photograph to the address given in the back of this book together with a stamped addressed envelope and I will arrange for the picture to be enlarged or reduced according to your request.)

Once the image is the right size, simply trace around the outline and transfer it to the sheet of blank graph paper supplied at the back of this book. Colour in the markings but leave out the finer details such as whiskers and eyes as it is better to embroider these afterwards. Draw a square around the graph with the same number of stitches and rows as the original graph of your selected jumper and knit up following the instructions as already set. **N.B.** You may wish to use oddments of different yarns to match the colours of your cat. If this is the case, be sure to double up fine yarns so that your tension remains even. Finally, work your graph in stocking stitch using the intarsia method (*see* Techniques, pages 9–10).

ABBREVIATIONS

alt	alternate(ly)	RS	right side(s)
beg	beginning	sl	slip
cm	centimetre(s)	ssk	slip 1 stitch, knit 1 stitch, pass slipped stitch over
cont	continue/continuing		
dec	decrease/decreasing	st(s)	stitch(es)
inc	increase/increasing	st st	stocking stitch
k	knit	tbl	through back of loop(s)
K1B	knit stitch through back loop	tog	together
MB	make bobble (*see* Techniques, page 11)	WS	wrong side(s)
		yo	place yarn over right-hand needle from back to front to make another st
p	purl		
psso	pass slipped stitch over		
rep	repeat		

TECHNIQUES

READING THE GRAPHS

Throughout the book explanatory graphs show the colour designs charted out, with stitch symbols added where necessary. Each square represents one stitch across, i.e., horizontally, and one row up, i.e., vertically. The graphs should be used in conjunction with the written instructions, which will tell you where and when to incorporate them. Any colours required or symbols used will be explained in the pattern. Always assume that you are working in stocking stitch unless otherwise instructed.

If you are not experienced in the use of graphs, remember that when you look at the flat page you are simply looking at a graphic representation of the right side of your piece of work, i.e., the smooth side of stocking stitch. For this reason, wherever possible, the graphs begin with a right side (RS) row so that you can see exactly what is going on as you knit. Knit rows are worked from right to left and purl rows from left to right.

TENSION

Knitting is simply a series of connecting loops, the construction of which is totally under the knitter's control. Tension or gauge is the term used to describe the actual stitch size — its width regulating the stitch tension measurement and its depth regulating the row tension measurement. Obtaining a specific tension is not a magical skill denied to all those but the initiated. It is a technicality, the controlling factor being the size of needles used by the knitter.

Since all knitting instructions are drafted to size using mathematical calculations relating to one tension and one tension only, that tension must be achieved before you start the work or you will have no control whatsoever over the size of the finished garment. *This is the most important rule of knitting.*

At the beginning of every pattern, a tension measurement will be given, using a specific stitch and needle size — e.g., 'using 5mm needles and measured over st st, 18 sts and 24 rows = 10cm square'. You must work a tension sample using exactly the same stitch and needle size as quoted. Cast on the number of stitches plus at least two extra because edge stitches, which do not give an accurate measurement, will not be counted. When it is complete, lay the tension sample or 'swatch' on a flat surface and, taking great care not to squash or stretch it, measure the tension, using a ruler and pins as shown.

If there are too few stitches, your tension is too loose. Use needles that are one size smaller to work another swatch. If there are too many stitches, your tension is too tight. Use needles that are one size larger to work another swatch.

Even if you have to change needle sizes several times, *keep working swatches until you get it right.* You save no time by skipping this stage of the work, because, if you do so, you risk having to undo an entire garment that has worked out to the wrong size. You may feel that a slight difference is negligible, but a tension measurement that is only a fraction of a stitch out per centimetre will result in inaccurate sizing because each fraction will have been multiplied by the number of centimetres across the work.

If you have had to change your needle size to achieve the correct tension for the main stitch and if other parts of the garment are worked on different sized needles, you must adjust these needles by the same ratio. For example, if you are using needles that are one size smaller than are quoted for

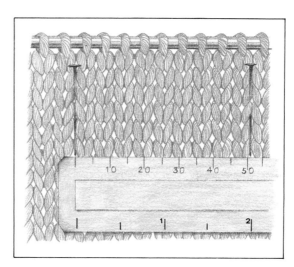

Use a ruler and pins to measure the gauge of a sample piece of knitting.

The wrong side (WS) of the work, showing stranding at the correct gauge.

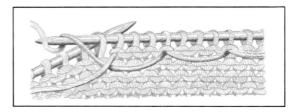

stocking stitch, use needles that are one size smaller than are quoted for the ribs.

I have intentionally omitted detailed reference to row tension because many people worry over this unnecessarily, changing their needle size even though they have achieved the correct stitch tension. Although important, row tension does vary considerably from yarn to yarn and knitter to knitter. If your stitch tension is absolutely accurate, your row tension will be only slightly out. Nevertheless, keep an eye on the work, especially when you are working something like a sleeve, which has been calculated in rows rather than centimetres, and compare it with the measurement diagram in case it becomes noticeably longer or shorter.

FAIRISLE

The technique of colour knitting called 'fairisle' is often confused with the traditional style of colour knitting that originated in the Fair Isles and took its name from those islands. Knitting instructions that call for the fairisle method do not necessarily produce a small-motifed repetitive pattern similar to that sported by the Prince of Wales in the Twenties — far from it, as can be seen from some of the patterns in this book.

The method referred to as fairisle knitting is when two colours are used across a row, with the one not in use being carried at the back of the work until it is next required. This is normally done by dropping one colour and picking up the other, using the right hand. If you are lucky enough to have mastered both the 'English' and 'Continental' methods of knitting, the yarns being used may be held simultaneously, one in the left hand, the other in the right hand. The instructions below, however, are limited to the more standard one-handed method and give the three alternative methods of dealing with the yarn not in use.

Stranding
Stranding is the term used to describe the technique by which the yarn not in use is simply left hanging at the back of the work until it is next needed. The yarn in use is then dropped and the carried yarn taken up, ready for use. This means that the strand, or 'float', thus produced on the

wrong side of the work has a direct pull on the stitches either side of it.

It is essential to leave a float long enough to span this gap without pulling the stitches out of shape and to allow the stitches in front of it to stretch and not to pucker on the right side of the work. It is preferable to go to the other extreme and leave a small loop at the back of the work rather than pull the float too tightly.

If the gap to be bridged by the float is wide, the strands produced may easily be caught and pulled when the garment is put on or taken off. This problem may be remedied by catching the floats down with a few stitches on the wrong side of the work at the finishing stage.

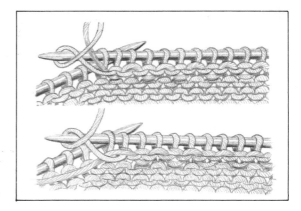

The wrong side of weaving, showing the up and down path of the carried yarn.

Weaving
With this method the yarn being carried is looped over or under the working yarn on every stitch, creating an up and down woven effect on the wrong side of the work. Since the knitter does not have to gauge the length of the floats, many people find that this is the easiest method of ensuring an even, accurate tension. Weaving does increase the chances of the carried colour showing through on to the right side of the work, however, and it tends to produce a far denser fabric, which is not always desirable when a thick fibre is being used.

Stranding and weaving
Combining the two methods of stranding

and weaving is invariably the most practical solution to the problem of working perfect fairisle. Most designs will have colour areas that will vary in the number of stitches. If the gap between areas of the same colour is only a few stitches, then stranding will suffice, but if the float produced will be too long, weave the carried yarn in every few stitches. Should you be unsure about the length of float to leave, slip your fingers under one. If you succeed with ease, the float is too long.

The most difficult aspect of fairisle knitting is getting the tension correct. This does not depend on the stitch size so much as on the way you treat the carried yarn. This is why, when working an all-over fairisle, you should always knit a tension sample in fairisle, not in main colour stocking stitch, as the weaving or stranding will greatly affect the finished measurement of the stitches. The most important rule to remember is that *the yarn being carried must be woven or stranded loosely enough to have the same degree of 'give' as the knitting itself.* Unless this is achieved, the resulting fabric will have no elasticity whatsoever and, in extreme examples, very tight floats will buckle the stitches so that they lie badly on the right side of the work.

If you are using the fairisle technique to work a colour motif on a single-colour background, keep the motif tension as close to the background tension as possible. If there is a great difference, the motif stitches will distort the image.

INTARSIA

Intarsia is the term used for the technique of colour knitting whereby each area of colour is worked using a separate ball of yarn, rather than carrying yarns from one area to another as in the fairisle technique. Any design that involves large blocks of isolated colour that are not going to be repeated along a row or required again a few rows later, should be worked in this way.

There are no limitations to the number of colours that may be used on any one row other than those imposed by lack of

patience and/or dexterity. Avoid getting into a tangle with too many separate balls of yarn hanging from the back of the work and remember that every time a new ball of yarn is introduced and broken off after use, two extra ends are produced that will have to be secured at the end of the day. When ends are left, always make sure that they are long enough to thread up so that they may be properly fastened with a pointed tapestry needle. Do this very carefully through the backs of the worked stitches to avoid distorting the design on the right side of the work. The ends that are left should never be knotted because they will make the wrong side of the work look extremely unsightly and they will invariably work themselves loose and create problems at a later stage.

If only a few large, regular areas of colour are being worked, avoid tangling the wool by laying the different balls of yarn on a table in front of you or keep them separate in individual jam jars or shoe-boxes. However, this requires careful turning at the end of every row so that the various strands do not become twisted.

The easiest method is to use small bobbins that hold each yarn separately and

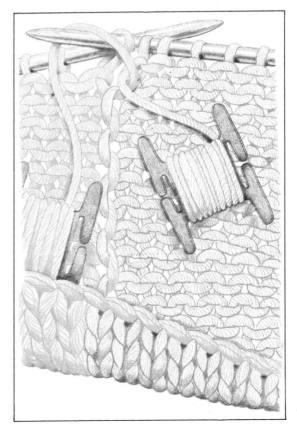

If you are using the intarsia method, twist the yarns firmly together when you change colours.

that hang at the back of the work. Such bobbins are available at most large yarn stores or they may be made at home out of stiff card. They come in a variety of shapes, but all have a narrow slit in them that keeps the wound yarn in place but allows the knitter to unwind a controlled amount as and when required. When winding yarn on to a bobbin, try to wind sufficient to complete an entire area of colour, but don't overwind, as heavy bobbins may pull stitches out of shape.

When you change colour from one stitch to another, it is essential that you twist the yarns around one another before dropping the old colour and working the first stitch in the new colour. This prevents a hole from forming. If it is not done, there is no strand to connect the last stitch worked in colour 'A' to the first stitch worked in colour 'B'. This twisting should also be done quite firmly to prevent a gap from appearing after the work has settled.

CASTING ON

The methods of casting on are too numerous to mention and choosing one is normally very much a matter of personal preference. When you are using cotton, however, the yarn itself must dictate the method used, because some methods will produce a cast-on edge that is far too uneven or 'frilly'. The technique described here will be familiar, in part, to most knitters since it involves the simple thumb method of casting on. By itself, this can produce an untidy edge, but with the addition of knitting into each stitch formed on the thumb, a neat, firm cast-on edge will be produced.

When you start to cast on, do not make a slip loop and put it on the needle, as is sometimes recommended, because this forms a noticeable knot when the work is completed. Instead, start straight in on the casting-on method, forming the first loop on the needle by slipping it off the thumb. When you come to form the next stitch, support the first loop at the back of the needle with the index finger of your left hand. This will stop the yarn twisting around the needle while you make the first proper stitch by knitting into the loop you have made around your thumb. These steps are repeated until the required number of stitches has been formed.

The work may now start straight away with row 1, which will be a wrong side (WS) row since it is the 'knot' side of the

A neat cast-on edge will result if you use the thumb method and, in addition, knit into each stitch.

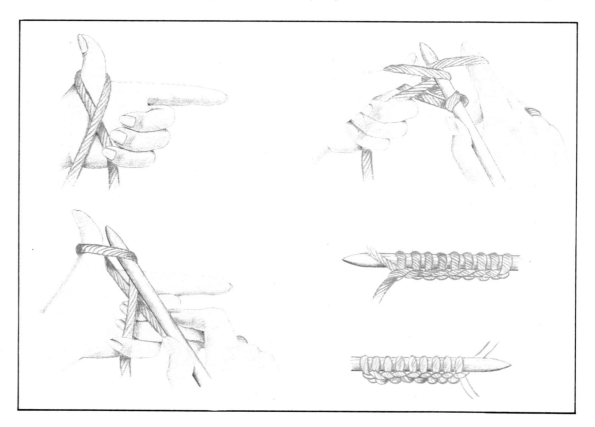

cast-on stitches.

MAKING A BOBBLE

Whenever the abbreviation MB appears in a pattern, it refers to a particular type of bobble, described below. There are numerous variations on the theme of bobble making, but in this book I have used just two, which, for ease of identification, I have called large and small. If worked on a right side (RS) row, the bobble will hang on the right side, if worked on a wrong side (WS) row, push it through on to the right side.

Large bobble
1. When the MB position on the row has been reached, make 5 stitches out of the

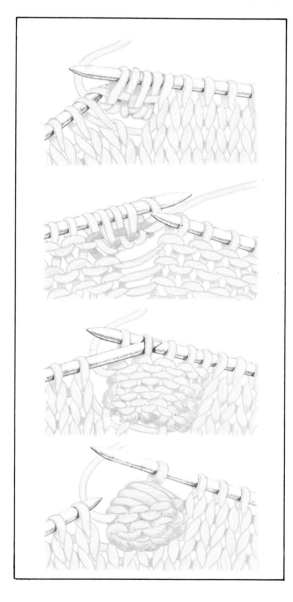

next one by knitting into its front, then its back, front, back and front again before slipping it off the LH needle.
2. Turn the work and knit these 5 stitches only.
3. Turn the work, purl 5 and repeat the last 2 rows.
4. Using the point of the left-hand needle, lift the bobble stitches, in order, over the first one on the right-hand needle, i.e., 2nd, 3rd, 4th and 5th, so that one stitch remains.

After completing the bobble, the work may continue as normal, the single stitch having been restored to its original position on the row.

Small bobble
This is made in exactly the same way as the large bobble, except that 4 stitches are made out of the 1, instead of 5. Rows 2 and 3 are worked but are not repeated.

TURNING

Turning is also called 'working short rows' since this is precisely what is being done. By turning the work in mid-row and leaving part of it unworked, shaping is created since one side of the work will have more rows than the other. If the work is then cast off, a sloping edge will result, making this method ideal for shoulder shaping instead of the more usual method of casting off groups of stitches to produce noticeable 'steps'. Turning is not advisable if you are working complicated stitches or colour patterns as working short rows will invariably throw them out.

Unfortunately, even when care is taken, there is a tendency for holes to form at the points where the work is turned. There is a method whereby these holes may be completely eliminated, and although this looks complicated at first, the finished effect is well worth the effort involved in mastering the technique.

This method may be used on right or wrong side rows. Here it has been illustrated on the right side of stocking stitch.

1. Knit to the point where turning is indicated, but before doing so bring the yarn to the front of the work and slip the next stitch from the left-hand to the right-hand needle.
2. Put the yarn to the back of the work and

The four steps in making a bobble are illustrated here. If you work a bobble on the wrong side (WS), push it through to the right side (RS) of your work.

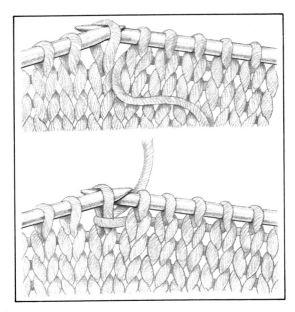

around it by putting the yarn forward and then back.

1. Slip this stitch from the left-hand to the right-hand needle, lifting the strand of the loop on to the right-hand needle along with the stitch.
2. Slip both the strand and the stitch back to the left-hand needle, straightening them as you do so.
3. Knit the stitch and strand together. Work to the next 'looped' stitch and repeat the process.

When this row is completed, the work may be continued as normal.

CABLES

A basic cable is simply a twist in the knitted fabric caused by working a small number of stitches out of sequence every few rows. This is done by slipping the stitches on to a needle and leaving them at the front or the back of the work while the next stitches on the left-hand needles are worked. The held stitches are then worked normally. The cable, worked in stocking stitch, will always be flanked by a few reversed stocking stitches to give it definition. Since it does involve a twist, however, cabled fabric will always have a tighter tension than one worked in plain stocking stitch, so take extra care when working a tension sample.

Cable needles are very short and double-ended. Some have a little kink in them to help keep the stitches in place while others are being worked. Use one that is a similar size to the needles being used for the main work and take care not to stretch or twist the stitches when moving them from needle to needle.

On the right side of the work, if the stitches are held to the front, the cable will cross from the right to the left. If the stitches are held at the back of the work, the cable will twist from the left to the right.

Front cross cable
1. (RS): work to the six stitches that are to be cabled. Slip the next three stitches on the left-hand needle on to the cable needle and leave them hanging at the front of the work.
2. Knit the next three stitches on the left-hand needle as normal.
3. Knit the three held stitches off the cable needle.

return the slipped stitch to the left-hand needle.
3. Now turn the work and purl to end.

Repeat the last three steps at every turning point.

All the stitches must now be worked across, so if the turned shaping is being worked immediately before casting off or knitting a seam, add an extra row. Work to the first stitch that has had a loop made

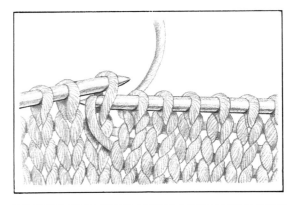

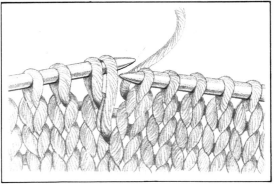

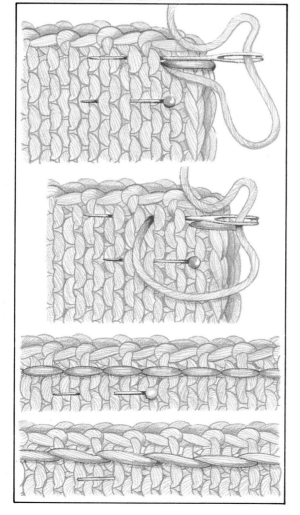

Repeat this twist wherever indicated in the instructions.

The same basic technique may be used to move a single stitch across a background of stocking stitch at a diagonal, rather than form a cable that moves up the work vertically.

Where the abbreviation cb2 is used, the first stitch is slipped on to the cable needle and left at the back of the work while the next stitch is knitted. The held stitch is then knitted off the cable needle. Cf2 is the same but with the cable needle left at the front of the work. On purl rows the abbreviations pcb2 and pcf2 are used to denote the same movement but in which the stitches are purled rather than knitted. In this way a continuous criss-cross line is formed.

SEAMS

After achieving the correct tension, the final sewing up of your knitting is the most important technique to master. It can make or break a garment, however carefully it may have been knitted. This is why the making up instructions after every set of knitting instructions should be followed exactly, especially to the type of seam to be used and the order in which the seams are to be worked.

Before starting any piece of work, always leave an end of yarn long enough to complete a substantial section, if not the whole length, of the eventual seam. After working a couple of rows, wind this up and pin it to the work to keep it out of the way. If required, also leave a sizable end when the work has been completed. This saves having to join in new ends that may well work loose, especially at stress points such as welts.

The secret of perfect-looking seams is uniformity and regularity of stitch. When joining two pieces that have been worked in the same stitch, they should be joined row for row, and all work should be pinned first to ensure an even distribution of fabrics. When joining work that has a design on both pieces, take great care to match the colours, changing the colour you are using to sew the seam where necessary.

Backstitch

Pin the two pieces of work together, right sides facing, making sure that the edges are absolutely flush. Always leave as narrow a

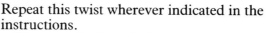
The front cross cable.

If you use backstitch to join a seam and you are starting at the very edge of the work, close the edges with an overstitch before beginning the row of backstitch.

When you use backstitch to join a seam, the finished seam should be perfectly straight; the drawings illustrate the appearance of the front (top) and the back (below) of the completed seam.

13

seam allowance as possible to reduce unnecessary bulk. It is essential that the line of backstitches is kept straight, using the lines of the knitted stitches as a guide. All the stitches should be identical in length, one starting immediately after the previous one has finished. On the side of the work facing you, the stitches should form a continuous, straight line. If the seam is starting at the very edge of the work, close the edges with an overstitch as shown. Now work the backstitch as follows:

1. Make a running stitch (maximum length 1cm), through both thicknesses of work.
2. Put the needle back into the work in exactly the same spot as before and make another running stitch twice as long.
3. Put the needle back into the work adjacent to the point where the previous stitch ended. Make another stitch the same length.

Keep repeating step 3 until the last stitch, which needs to be half as long to fill in the final gap left at the end of the seam.

By keeping the stitch line straight and by pulling the yarn fairly firmly after each stitch, no gaps should appear when the work is opened out and the seam pulled apart.

This seam is suitable for lightweight yarns or when an untidy selvedge has been worked.

Flat seam

This seam is a slight contradiction in terms since its working involves an oversewing action, but when the work is opened out it will do so completely and lie quite flat, unlike a backstitched seam.

Use a blunt-ended tapestry needle to avoid splitting the knitted stitches. Pin both pieces right sides together and hold the work as shown. The needle is placed through the very edge stitch on the back piece and then through the very edge stitch on the front piece. The yarn is pulled through and the action repeated, with the needle being placed through exactly the same part of each stitch every time. Always work through the edge stitch only. By taking in more than this, a lumpy, untidy seam that will never lie flat will be produced.

When two pieces of stocking stitch are to

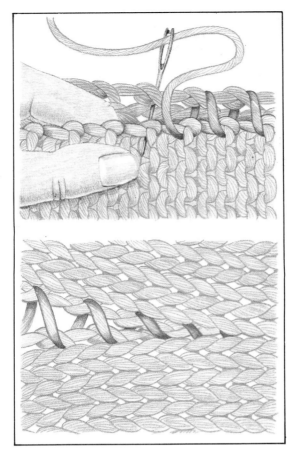

be joined with a flat seam, do not work any special selvedge such as knitting every edge stitch. Just work the edge stitches normally but as tightly as possible, using only the tip of your needle. When you come to work the seam, place the needle behind the knots of the edge stitches and not the looser strands that run between the knots, since these will not provide a firm enough base for the seam, which will appear gappy when opened out.

Flat seams are essential for heavy-weight yarns where a backstitch would create far too much bulk. They should also be used for attaching buttonbands, collars and so forth, where flatness and neatness are essential.

Borders, welts, cuffs and any other part of a garment where the edge of the seam will be visible should be joined with a flat seam, even if the remainder of the garment is to have a backstitched seam. Start with a flat seam until the rib/border is complete and then change over to a backstitch, taking in a tiny seam allowance at first and then smoothly widening it without making a sudden inroad into the work.

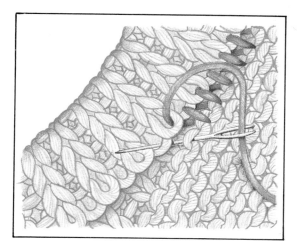

Use slip stitch to hold a double neckband in position and (left below) to attach a pocket to a garment.

Slip stitch

Where one piece of work is to be placed on top of another, for example when turning in a double neckband, folding over a hem or attaching the edges of pocket borders, a slip stitch should be used.

When turning in a neckband that has been cast off, the needle should be placed through the cast-off edge and then through the same stitch but on the row where it was initially knitted up. It is essential to follow the line of the stitch to avoid twisting the neckband. By repeating the action, the visible sewn stitch runs at a diagonal.

The same rule applies when sewing down a neckband that has not been cast off but that has had its stitches held on a thread. The only difference is that the needle is placed through the actual held stitch, thus securing it. When each stitch has been slip stitched down, the thread may be removed. This method allows for a neckband with more 'give' than one that has been cast off.

On pocket borders, use the line of stitches on the main work as a guide to produce a perfectly straight vertical line of stitches. Place the needle through one strand of the main work stitch and then behind the knot of the border edge stitch, as for a flat seam.

KNITTED SHOULDER SEAMS

This method of joining is perfect for shoulders on which no shaping has been worked or on which the shaping has been worked by turning rows, as described on pages 11–12. It creates an extremely neat, flat seam.

Since the two pieces to be joined must be worked stitch for stitch, they must both have exactly the same number of stitches. Even though the pattern specifies that you should have a certain number of stitches at this point, it is wise to double check the number you actually have on your needles, since it is very easy to lose or gain the odd stitch accidentally along the way.

The technique itself involves the use of three needles. The stitches from the front and back are held on their respective needles, both of which are held in the left hand, while the right hand holds a third, larger, needle, which helps to prevent the cast-off stitches from becoming too tight. Holding more than one needle in the hand and trying to work through two stitches at a time without dropping them can seem awkward at first, but, with a little practice, it will feel like normal knitting.

The needles are held with the right sides of the work facing one another and with the stitches lined up at corresponding intervals on the front and back needles.

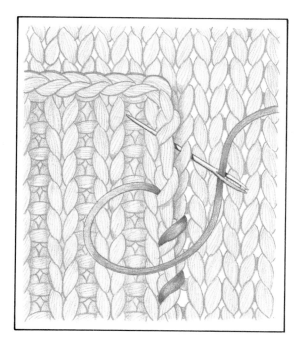

1. The point of the right-hand needle is put through the first stitch on the front needle and the first stitch on the back needle, with exactly the same action as a normal knit stitch but going through both simultaneously.
2. A loop is pulled through to form a single stitch on the right-hand needle, the old

The diagrams illustrate the
three steps involved in
knitting shoulder seams
together. You must always
have exactly the same number
of stitches on the two pieces
that are to be joined in this
way.

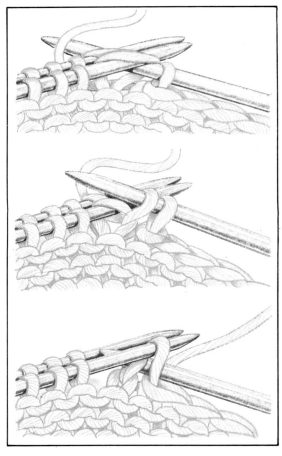

When Swiss darning, use a
yarn of the same thickness as
the knitting and follow the
path of the knitted stitches.

stitches being slipped off the left-hand
needle.

3. These two steps are repeated so that
   there are two stitches on the right-hand
   needle. The second stitch is then lifted
   over the first, as in normal casting off.

Step 3 should be repeated across all the
stitches to be knitted together until one loop
remains on the right-hand needle. Pull the
yarn through this to secure.

When knitting together a shoulder seam
on a garment where no neck shaping has
been worked and the neck stitches have not
been cast off, the back stitches may be dealt
with altogether. By starting to work the first
shoulder together from the armhole to the
neck edge, the back neck stitches may then
be cast off (if the pattern requires that they
are cast off), without breaking the yarn,
which may then be used to knit together the
second shoulder seam.

Normally worked on the inside of the
work to create an extremely neat, flat and
durable seam on the right side of the work,
a knitted seam may be worked with the
wrong sides of the knitting facing one
another. This creates a decorative ridge on
the right side of the work.

SWISS DARNING

This is the most straightforward method of
embroidery that may be worked on knitted
fabrics since it exactly replicates knitted
stitches. For this reason Swiss darning is
sometimes called 'duplicate stitch'. By
following the path of the knitted stitch with
a contrasting colour, it is possible to create
a variety of designs that have the
appearance of being worked as a complicated fairisle, although they have, more
simply, been added afterwards. For knitters
who are not too confident with colour
techniques, this is a very useful adjunct to
their knitting skills.

When Swiss darning, always use a yarn
of the same thickness as the knitting so that
it will cover the stitch beneath it but not
create an embossed effect. Use a blunt-
ended tapestry needle to avoid splitting the
knitted stitches as you embroider. The
tension of the embroidered stitches must be
kept exactly the same as the work that is
providing the base so that they sit properly
and do not pucker the work. The tension is
regulated by how tightly the embroidery

yarn is pulled through the work at each stage. Take great care when joining in and securing yarn ends on the wrong side of the work so that the stitches in the area do not become distorted.

BUTTONHOLES

A badly worked buttonhole can spoil the look of a garment, pulling the buttonband out of shape and looking loopy. It is also of no practical use if it is worked too tightly or, as more often happens, too loosely so that the buttons are not held.

Because finding buttons that are perfectly suited to the garment you are working can prove difficult, it is advisable to find the buttons before you work the buttonholes. The buttonhole size may then be adjusted slightly to suit the buttons rather than the other way round. The adjustment is easily made by casting off one or two stitches more or less than stated in the instructions — provided, of course, that there are enough stitches across the buttonband to accommodate such an alteration.

All the buttonholes used in this book are of the most basic, horizontal variety, worked over two rows. On the first row the required number of stitches is cast off at intervals corresponding to the distance between each button. On the next row the same number of stitches is cast on, immediately above those that were cast off on the previous row. If you use the thumb method of casting on, the first cast-on stitch often forms a loop unless it is worked with the yarn pulled very tightly on the needle. Alternatively, the work may be turned so that a two-needle method of casting on may be used to replace the cast-off stitches before turning the work back again and continuing the row normally until the next buttonhole point is reached.

When you work a buttonhole across ribbing, which is the most usual practice, keep in pattern throughout, although the casting off should be either knitwise or purlwise to give a firmer finish than a ribbed cast-off edge, which will be too elastic. Remember, all buttonholes should be a fraction too tight for their buttons when first completed, to allow for the inevitable stretching that occurs as a result of wear and tear.

EMBROIDERY

To achieve the detail necessary for the facial features of some of the cats incorporated into the garments, simple embroidery stitches have been added after the knitting has been completed. You may find it helpful to sketch roughly on to the fabric, using tailor's chalk or lines of very small pins, the position and outline of the embroidery.

Satin stitch
Satin stitch is used to 'in-fill' areas such as eyes. It is formed by working straight stitches, very close to one another, over the length of the area to be covered.

Backstitch
Outlines are worked in backstitch, which should be worked in exactly the same way as the stitch used for seams (*see* page 12). When you are working a curve, try to make very small stitches to ensure a continuous line.

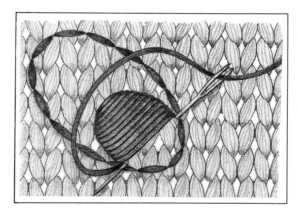

When you embroider facial features such as eyes use satin stitch for solid areas and backstitch for outlines.

KNITTING UP STITCHES

The term 'picking up' stitches is sometimes used instead of 'knitting up' stitches, but it is rather a misleading phrase since it implies that the stitches are simply strands that have been pulled out around the edge of the work. This should never be done, for it produces uneven and untidy loops. The correct method is to use new yarn to create brand new stitches through the edge of the existing knitted fabric. This produces tidy, uniform stitches, and allows you to control the positioning of them.

As with working perfect flat seams, the preparation — i.e., the actual knitting — is the most important part of knitting up stitches. A firmly and neatly worked edge is essential for tidy knitting up. Always work edge stitches tightly, and if shaping has been worked — around a neckline, for instance — any decreases or increases should be worked one or two stitches in from the edge stitch wherever the pattern will allow. In this way the irregular, stretched stitches of the shaping are out of the way and the normally worked edge stitches can form the basis of the new stitches. Each new stitch should emerge from behind the knot of the edge stitch as this is the firmest part of the stitch. The strand between the knots will tend to stretch and should be used only when there is no alternative.

If you are working a colour pattern on a main colour, stop the pattern short a few stitches in from the edge so that the last few stitches are worked in main colour only. Knitting up from stitches of various colours will create an untidy line. When you are completing a piece of work that is to have stitches knitted up at a later stage, leave the yarn attached so that it may be used when required and so that you do not have to join in a new end of yarn, which will have to be secured.

When a pattern states exactly how many stitches are to be knitted up, if you are to work them in a stitch for which you have not worked a separate tension sample — e.g., rib when the pattern has required you to work a tension sample over stocking stitch — it is worthwhile to work a few knitted-up stitches as a test before beginning the knitting-up proper since rib tension varies compared with stocking stitch.

If you find it difficult to distribute the number of stitches that are to be knitted up, divide your work into halves and then into quarters (and even eighths if it is a long edge), and mark these points with pins. Apportion the number of stitches equally among these sections. If they do not divide equally, use any extra stitches where they might be needed, such as at seam edges. Never distribute the stitches as you go along as this will invariably result in an uneven effect, with some areas bunched

with too many stitches and others stretched with too few.

Once the edge has been prepared, hold the work with the right side towards you. Hold the yarn at the back of the work so that the stitches may be pulled through to the front. This may be done either with the needle you intend to use for the first row or, more easily, with a crochet hook. Use a crochet hook that will slip easily through the base stitch to catch the yarn and pull it through to the right side of the work where it is then slipped onto the needle holding the new stitches. Pull the yarn tight. The holding needle should be one or two sizes smaller than the size quoted for the actual knitting up to reduce the stitch size on the first row, thus creating a neater finish. Change to the correct needle size on your second row. The first row of a band or border that is to be ribbed may also be either knitted or purled as this, too, creates a smaller stitch than an initial row of ribbing. Knitting this row with the right side facing you gives a smooth, inconspicuous row. If you purl this row, a ridge will be formed on the right side of the work, which will neaten the knit-up edge in a more ornamental way. Ribbing should then continue as normal.

If stitches are held between two areas of knitted-up stitches, as they may often be at the centre front edge of a crew neck, slip these stitches onto another needle and then knit them onto the holding needle. This will save you from having to break the yarn; slip the held stitches onto the holding needle and join in the yarn again to knit up further stitches. It is also advisable to knit up a stitch from the loop at the beginning and the end of any set of stitches that have been cast off or are on a holder. These are stress points and often become stretched, and an extra stitch will prevent a hole forming.

If you are using a set of double-pointed needles to knit around some necklines, the same rules apply, but the stitches that are knitted up must be equally distributed among the number of needles in use, leaving one needle free for the working.

CARING FOR YOUR GARMENTS

Given the time and effort involved in knitting your garment, a few basic rules should be followed to ensure that it retains its shape and good looks.

All of the garments in this book should be stored flat and should never be hung. While a luke-warm soap solution is quite acceptable for hand-washing wool or mohair garments, dry-cleaning them will ensure that they last longer. Hand-knitted garments should always be dried flat over a frame. After washing a cotton-yarn garment, you should spin it to get rid of the excess moisture which can easily spoil its shape. Never tumble-dry garments made from natural fibres. If you are concerned about the unavoidable shedding properties of mohair when it is washed, dry-cleaning is the best method of safeguarding your garment.

Detail from the back of Priscilla Mohair Coat (page 43).

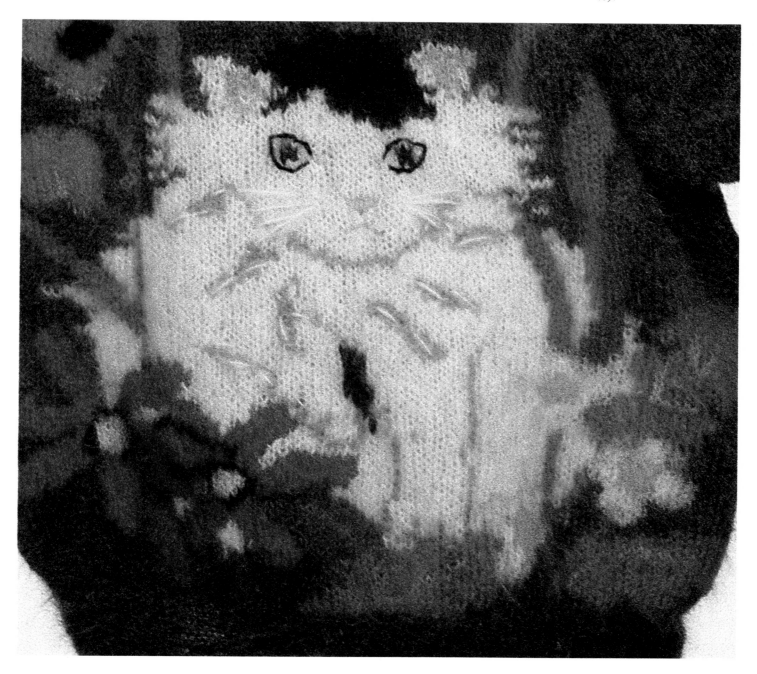

RUMPLETEAZER JUMPER AND LEGGINGS

A double-knitting wool jumper and leggings worked using the intarsia method (*see* Techniques, pages 9–10).

Materials
Jumper: Melinda Coss DK – main colour (bilberry): 450gm; raspberry: 100gm; platinum, purple haze, magenta, orange, cream, brown, pink, emerald and gold: less than 50gm of each.
Leggings: Melinda Coss DK – black: 400gm.

Needles
One pair of 3¼mm and one pair of 4mm needles.

Tension
Using 4mm needles and measured over st st, 21 sts and 27 rows = 10cm square. Ribs worked on 3¼mm needles.

N.B. The following symbols are used to indicate that bobbles should be worked in the appropriate colour: triangles–magenta; circles–emerald; crosses–orange (*see* Techniques, page 11).

JUMPER

Front

Using 3¼mm needles and bilberry, cast on 100 sts. Work in k2, p2 rib for 26cm, inc 14 sts evenly across last row of rib. Change to 4mm needles and begin to follow graph in stocking stitch until row 112 is complete.
Shape neck: k51. Sl remaining 63 sts onto a spare needle. Turn, p back the 51 sts. Working on this last set of sts only, k47, sl 1, k1, psso, k2, turn, p back 50 sts. Next row: k46, sl 1, k1, psso, k2, turn, p back 49 sts. Cont to dec in this fashion until 45 sts remain. Work without further shaping for 16 rows. Sl remaining 45 sts onto a spare needle. Go back to the sts held for the second side and sl the first 12 sts onto a stitch holder. Rejoin yarn at inner edge of remaining sts, k to end. Turn, p back, then begin shaping as for other side. When shaping is complete, work 16 rows straight. Place remaining 45 sts on a spare needle.

Back

Work as for front, following graph for back. Cont without shaping until 135 rows have been worked. **Shape neck:** k45 sts. Turn; work 3 rows on these 45 sts, break off yarn, hold these 45 sts on a spare needle. Slip centre 24 sts onto a holder, rejoin yarn to neck edge on remaining sts. Work 4 rows. Leave sts on a holder.

Sleeves

Using 3¼mm needles and bilberry, cast on 36 sts and work in k2, p2 rib for 15cm, inc 16 sts evenly across last row of rib (52 sts). Change to 4mm needles and cont in st st only, inc 1 st at each end of every 4th row until you have 96 sts. Work without further shaping until sleeve measures 49cm. Cast off.

Neckband

With RS of front and back facing, knit right shoulder seams together. Using 3¼mm needles and bilberry, pick up and knit 26 sts down left front neck, 12 sts from centre front, 26 sts up right front neck, 4 sts down right back, 24 sts held for centre back and 4 sts down left back (96 sts). Work 8 rows in k2, p2 rib. Cast off loosely.

Making up

Knit 2nd set of shoulder seams together. Join sleeves to body using a fine backstitch. Join back, front and sleeve seams using a flat seam. Join neck rib with an invisible seam.

LEGGINGS

(Worked in two pieces: left/right leg)

Ankle rib

Using 3¼mm needles, cast on 50 sts. Work in k1, p1 rib for 16 rows. Change to 4mm needles and **commence leg:** work in st st, beginning with a knit row and inc 1 st at each end of every 6th row until you have completed 180 rows, excluding rib (110 sts).

Crotch

Cast off 10 sts at beg of the next 2 rows (90 sts). Work 64 rows for rise.

Waistband

Change to 3¼mm needles and work in k1, p1 rib for 16 rows. Cast off loosely.

Work second leg as first.

Making up

Using a flat seam, join leg and rise seams. Turn waistband hem inwards and slip stitch into position, leaving a gap for the elastic to be inserted. Using a safety-pin, thread the elastic through, overlap the ends and backstitch together.

The graph opposite is for the front of the jumper. The symbols ▲, × and ● indicate that a bobble should be made at this point (see Techniques page 11). The colours are given under Materials on page 21.

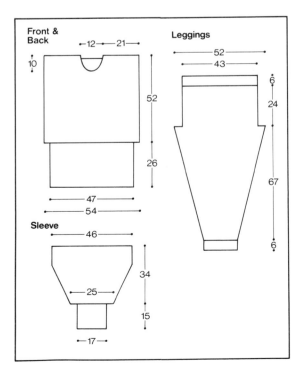

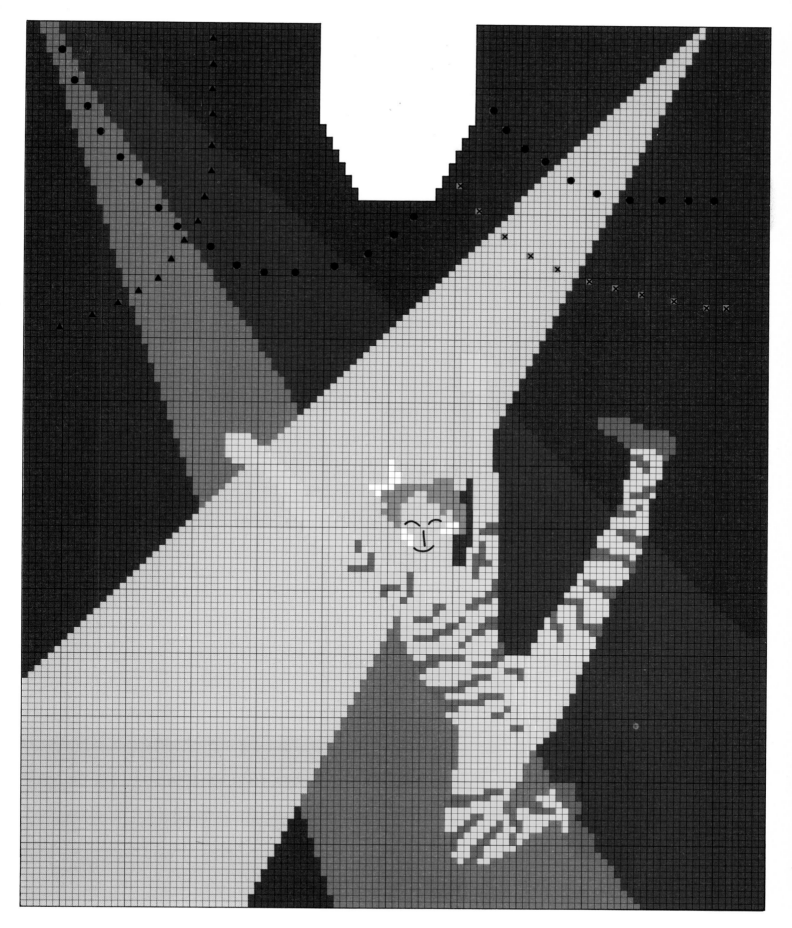

23

The graph opposite is for the back of the jumper. The symbols ▲, × and ● indicate that a bobble should be made at this point (see Techniques page 11).

25

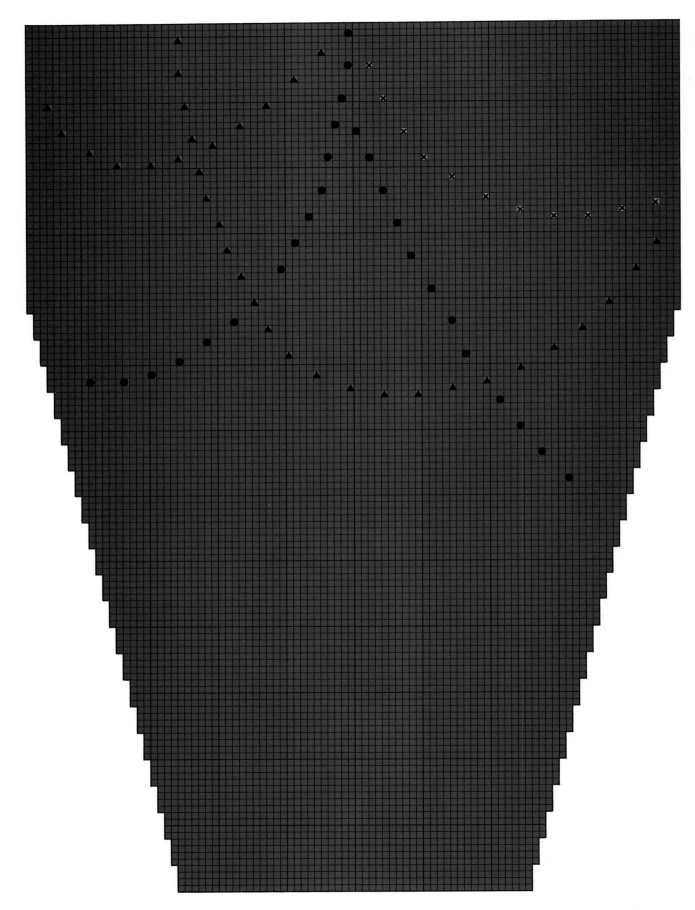

The graph opposite is for the sleeves. The position of the bobbles is shown by the symbols ▲, × and ● (see **Materials** *page 21 for colours.)*

'CATS' JUMPER

Materials
Melinda Coss DK
mercerized cotton – slate:
1kg; black, white and
yellow: less than 50gm of
each.

Needles
1 pair of 3¼mm and 1
pair of 3¾mm needles.

Tension
Using 3¾mm needles
and measured over st st,
24 sts and 30 rows =
10cm square. Ribs
worked on 3¼mm
needles.

For lovers of the show *Cats*, this jumper is
a must. Worked in double-knitting cotton
using the intarsia method (*see* Techniques,
pages 9–10), the big baggy shape is suitable
for men and women.

Front
Using 3¼mm needles and main colour, cast
on 120 sts. Work in k1, p1 rib for 10cm,
inc 18 sts evenly across last row of rib (138
sts). Change to 3¾mm needles and work in
stocking stitch in slate only for 36 rows.
Next row: begin reading graph 1, positioning it as follows: k52, k first row of
graph, k52. Cont with graph in this
position until it is complete. Work 64 rows
in main colour only.

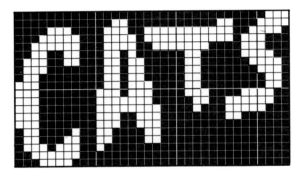

Next row: begin reading graph 2, positioning as follows: k25, k first row of graph,
k25. Cont with graph in this position until
it is complete. Work 16 rows in main
colour.
Shape neck: k56, place these sts on a spare
needle, sl centre 26 sts onto a stitch holder,
rejoin yarn, k56 to end. Working on this

last set of sts only, dec 1 st at neck edge on
the next 11 alt rows. Work 8 rows without
shaping, sl remaining 45 sts onto a spare
needle. Repeat for other side.

Back
Work as for front in main colour only until
back matches front to shoulder. Place a
marker on the 45th st at each end for shoulders. Hold stitches on a spare needle.

Sleeves
Using 3¼mm needles and main colour, cast
on 56 sts and work in k1, p1 rib for 6cm,
inc 4 sts evenly across last row of rib (60
sts). Change to 3¾mm needles and cont in
st st, inc 1 st at each end of every 4th row
until there are 124 sts. Work without
further shaping until sleeve measures 52cm
from start. Cast off loosely.

Neckband
Knit one shoulder seam together (*see*
Techniques, page 15). Using 3¼mm
needles, pick up and knit the 48 sts held for
centre back, 30 sts down one side of front,
26 sts held for centre front and 30 sts up
other side of front (134 sts). Work in k1, p1
rib for 6cm. Cast off.

Making up
Knit second shoulder seam together. Turn
neckband inwards and slip stitch cast-off
edge to pick-up edge. Join sleeves to
jumper, then join sleeve and body seams
using a flat seam.

*Graph 1 (right) is for the
word 'cats'. Start reading the
graph at the bottom
right-hand corner.*

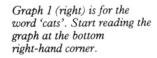

*Graph 2 (below) is for the
spotlights. Start reading the
graph at the bottom
right-hand corner.*

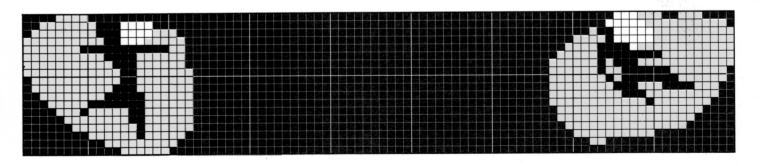

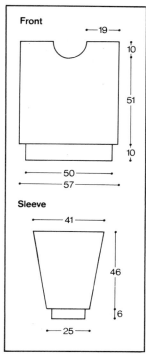

BRICK-WALL CAT JACKET

Materials
Melinda Coss DK wool – silver: 350gm; scarlet: 150gm; black, bilberry, coffee, white, cream, rust, camel, blue and yellow: less than 50gm of each; a few scraps of pink.

Needles
One pair of 3¾mm and one pair of 4½mm needles; one 3¾mm circular needle.

Tension
Using 4½mm needles and worked over brick-wall pattern, 26 sts and 30 rows = 10cm square. Ribs worked on 3¾mm needles.

This jaunty double-breasted jacket in double-knitting wool is knitted in an interesting checkered stitch showing a cat design. The pattern is worked using the intarsia method (*see* Techniques, pages 9–10).

Brick-wall pattern
A = silver; B = scarlet.
Row 1, A: knit.
Row 2, A: purl.
Row 3, B: k3, *sl 1, k5* to end.
Row 4, B: k3, *sl slipped st of previous row, k5*, rep to last 4 sts, sl 1, k3.
Row 5, B: p3, *sl slipped st of previous row, p5, *rep to last 4 sts, sl 1, p3.
Row 6, B: work as for row 4.
Row 7, A: knit.
Row 8, A: purl.
Row 9, B: *sl 1 st, k5*, rep to last st, sl 1.
Row 10, B: *sl slipped st of previous row, k5*, rep to last st, sl 1.
Row 11, B: *sl st, p5*, rep to last st, sl 1.
Row 12, B: work as for row 10.
Repeat from row 1.

Right front
Using 3¾mm needles and A, cast on 50 sts. K2, p2 rib for 6 rows. Change to 4½mm needles and begin brick-wall pattern.
Row 1, A: knit. Row 2, B: purl. Row 3, B:

k1. Complete as shown. Row 4: work as shown to last st, k1. Cont following the pattern, working an extra stitch at beg of RS rows and at end of WS rows. Work until the 12 pattern rows are complete. Begin working graph 1, using A and st st only. Cont graph until complete, then cont in brick-wall pattern, beginning on row 1 as set for 10 rows.
Shape neck: cont in pattern, dec 1 st at beg of the next row and the 17 following 3rd rows. When the neck shaping is complete, 32 sts will remain. Work 10 rows without shaping.
Shape shoulders: next row (WS): cast off 16 sts at beg of this row and the next alt row.

Left front
Work as for right front, but use graph 2 and reverse all shapings.

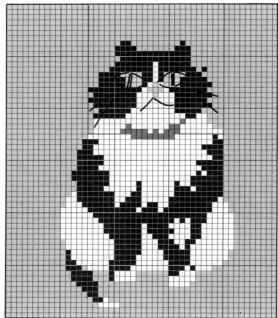

Graph 1 (right) shows the cat design for the right front of the jacket (see photo on page 33). The red line indicates the design used for the egg-cosies on page 87.

Graph 2 (far right) shows the cat design for the left front of the jacket. The red line indicates the design used for the egg-cosies on page 87.

Graph 3 is on page 33.

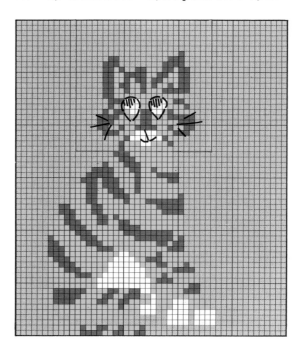

Back
Using 3¾mm needles, cast on 127 sts and work in k1, p1 rib. (Row 1: k1, *p1, k1, rep from * to end. Row 2: p1, *k1, p1, rep from * to end). Rep these 2 rows twice more. Change to 4½mm needles and work in brick-wall pattern for 12 rows. Commence following graph 3, working in st st and A until graph is complete. Cont in

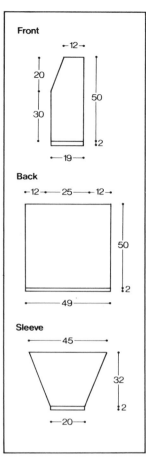

Front

12

20

30

50

2

19

Back

12 · 25 · 12

50

2

49

Sleeve

45

32

2

20

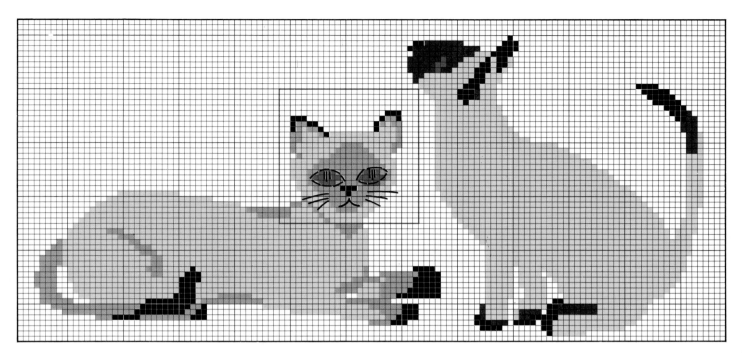

brick-wall pattern until back matches front to shoulder shaping. Still working in brick-wall pattern, cast off 16 sts at beg of the next 4 rows. Leave remaining 63 sts on a holder.

Sleeves (Both alike)

Using 3¾mm needles, cast on 53 sts. Work in k1, p1 rib for 10cm. Change to 4½mm needles and work in brick-wall pattern as follows:

Row 1, A: knit. Row 2, A: purl. Row 3, B: inc 1, k2. Work row as shown, k2, inc 1. Cont in pattern, incorporating the 2 extra sts at each end of every row and inc 1 st at each end of every 3rd row until there are 117 sts. Cast off loosely in A.

Making up

Join shoulder and side seams, using invisible seams throughout and taking care to match pattern.

Collar

Using a 3¾mm circular needle and A, and with RS of work facing you, pick up and knit 149 sts from bottom of right front to top neckline, 63 sts held for back of neck and 150 sts down left front (362 sts). Row 1: k2, *p2, k2, rep from * to end. Row 2: p2, *k2, p2, rep from * to end. Repeat these 2 rows twice more.
Work buttonholes: rib 11, cast off 4 sts. Rib 27, cast off 4 sts. Rib 27, cast off 4 sts,

rib to end. On return row, cast on 4 sts over each of the 3 buttonholes. Cont in 2 × 2 rib for a further 26 rows. Repeat buttonhole rows. Rib for a further 10 rows. Cast off.

Graph 3 shows the design on the back of the jacket.

CAT AND MOUSE JUMPER

Materials
Melinda Coss aran-weight wool – royal blue: 400gm; yellow: 400gm; black: 50gm; white: 50gm.

Needles
One pair of 4mm and one pair of 5mm needles; one 4mm circular needle.

Tension
Using 5mm needles and measured over st st, 17 sts and 22 rows = 10cm square. Ribs worked on 4mm needles.

An aran-weight boxy jumper with collar and lots of pockets. Worked using the intarsia method (*see* Techniques, pages 9–10).

Pocket-linings (Make 2 yellow and 1 blue)
Using 5mm needles, cast on 25 sts. Work 30 rows of st st and leave on spare needles.

Front
Using 4mm needles and blue, cast on 98 sts. K1, p1 rib, working 4 rows in blue, 4 rows in yellow and 4 rows in blue. Change to 5mm needles and begin following graph in st st, starting with a knit row. Work straight, following graph until you have completed 94 rows.
Make pocket: row 95: k10, sl 25 sts onto a spare needle, k to end. Return row: p55, p across sts held for blue pocket-lining, p to end. Cont following graph to row 121.
Shape neck: row 122: p46, cast off 6, sl first 46 sts onto a spare needle, p to end. Working on the last set of sts only, k back to neck edge. Cast off 5 sts at beg of next row and the following alt row. Cast off 4 sts at beg of next alt row and 3 sts on the following 2 alt rows. Work 1 row, sl remaining 26 sts onto a holder. Rejoin yarn to neck edge and rep shaping for the other side of neck.

Back
Work as for front, ignoring the cat motif until you have completed 44 rows of graph.
Pocket row: k59, sl 25 sts onto a holder, k to end. On return row, work across yellow pocket-lining in place of the held sts. Cont as for front, omitting the top pocket and the neck shaping until 131 rows have been completed.
Shape neck: p24, turn, k24, sl these 24 sts onto a stitch holder, break off yarn and rejoin to remaining stitches. Cast off centre 50 sts. Work to end, turn, work one row, sl remaining 24 sts onto a holder.

Right sleeve
Using 4mm needles and blue, cast on 50 sts. Work in k1, p1 rib, working 4 rows in blue, 4 rows in yellow and 4 rows in blue. Change to 5mm needles and yellow and work in st st, inc 1 st at each end of every 4th row until you have 100 sts. At the same time, when you have completed 50 rows,
make pocket: row 51: p25, sl centre 25 sts onto a holder, p to end. On return row, work across your last pocket-lining in place of held sts. Once you have increased the sleeve to 100 sts, work 4 rows straight and cast off loosely.

Left sleeve
Using 4mm needles and yellow, cast on 50 sts. Work in k1, p1 rib, working 4 rows in yellow, 4 rows in blue and 4 rows in yellow. Change to 5mm needles and cont as for right sleeve, but using blue only and omitting the pocket.

Pocket tops
(All alike but starting blue pockets with blue and yellow pockets with yellow)
Using 4mm needles, pick up the stitches held for pocket top and work in k1, p1 rib for 4 rows. Cast off. Stitch pockets into position and sew pocket-top edges to jumper.
Place front and back RS together and knit shoulder seams together.

Neckband
Using a 4mm circular needle and yellow, pick up and knit 84 sts evenly around the neck. Work in rounds of k1, p1 rib for 4cm. Cast off loosely in rib and turn neckband inwards. Slip stitch cast-off edge to pick-up edge.

Collar
Using 4mm needles and blue, cast on 120

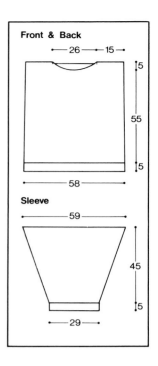

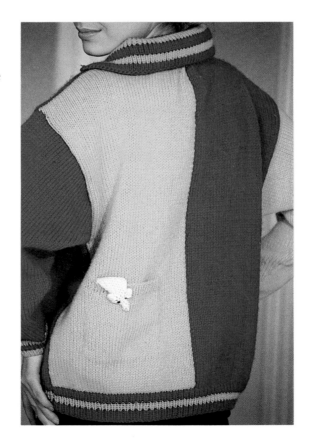

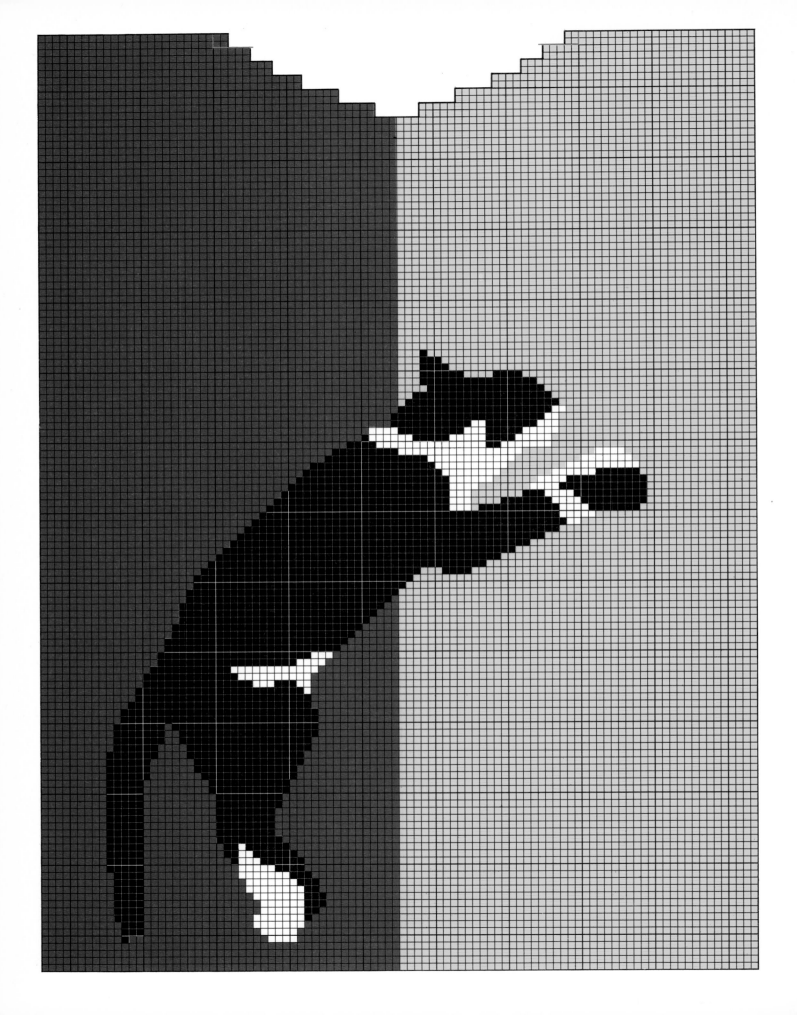

sts and work in k1, p1 rib, changing colour every 4 rows until you have completed 32 rows (8 stripes). Cast off loosely in rib, sew collar onto inside seam of neck.

Making up
Join sleeves to body using narrow backstitch. Using a flat seam, join sleeve and body seams.

Mice (Make 3)
Using 5mm needles and white, cast on 18 sts. Work 2 rows in st st, then cont in st st, dec 1 st at each end of the next row and every alt row until you have 8 sts.

Make ears: next row (WS): p2. **K4 from 1, turn, k4, turn, sl 1, p1, psso, *p1, pass st over, rep from * once more, p2, rep from **. Cont working in st st, dec 1 st at each end of every alt row until you have 2 sts. K2 tog, fasten off.
With pink wool, make a knot on the point of the triangle for nose. Using black, make 2 knots 1cm up from the nose and 1cm apart for the eyes. Stitch side seams together and sew along bottom edge. To make whiskers, thread a small length of white wool through the head and knot either side, trim yarn and separate. Sew mice into pockets on front, sleeve and back.

The graph opposite shows the design for the front of the Cat and Mouse jumper.

'CATASTROPHE' SWEATER

An aran-weight, crew-necked sweater, worked using the intarsia method (*see* Techniques, pages 9–10).

Front
Using 6mm needles and black, cast on 100 sts.
Row 1: k2 black, p2 white, rep to end.
Repeat these 2 rows until rib measures 7cm. Change to main colour and begin following graph in st st for 75 rows. **Shape armholes:** cast off 2 sts at beg of next 2 rows.* Cont without further shaping until 120 rows are complete.
Shape neck: k42, sl next 54 sts onto a spare needle and work on these first 42 sts only. Turn, cast off 5 sts, p to end. Dec 1 st at neck edge on next 6 rows (31 sts). Work 2 rows. Sl remaining 31 sts onto a stitch holder.
Return to the stitches held for the other side of neck. Sl first 12 sts onto a stitch holder, rejoin yarn at neck edge, k to end, turn, p to end, turn, cast off 5 sts, k to end, turn. Dec 1 st at neck edge on the next 6 rows. Work 1 row, place remaining stitches on a spare needle.

Back
Work as for front to *. Work without further shaping until 124 rows are complete. K41, sl remaining 55 sts onto a spare needle, working on this first set of 41 sts only, turn, cast off 6 sts, p to end. Dec 1 st at neck edge on next 3 rows. Work 2 rows. Leave remaining 32 sts on a spare needle. Return to the stitches held for other side of neck. Sl first 13 sts onto a stitch holder, rejoin yarn to remaining sts. K to end, turn, p to end, turn, cast off 6 sts at beg of the next row, then dec 1 st at neck edge on next 3 rows. Work 1 row. Place remaining sts on a spare needle.

Materials
Melinda Coss aran-weight wool – red: 550gm; black: 100gm; white: 200gm; pink: less than 10gm.

Needles
One pair of 5½mm and one pair of 6mm needles.

Tension
Using 6mm needles and measured over st st, 16 sts and 20 rows = 10cm square.

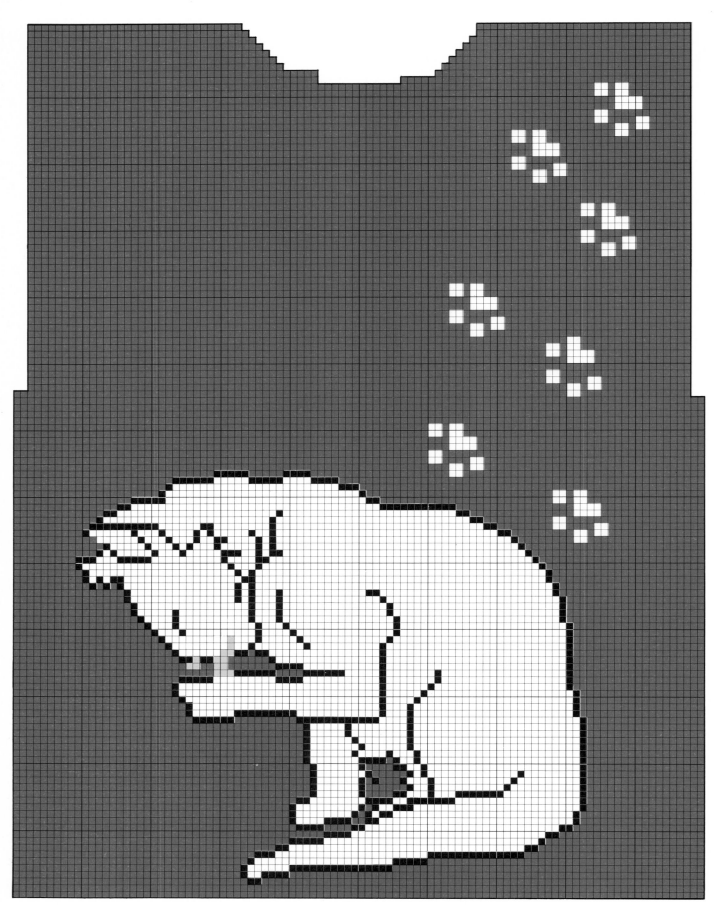

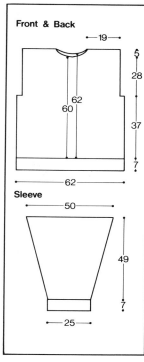

The graph opposite is for the front of the sweater.

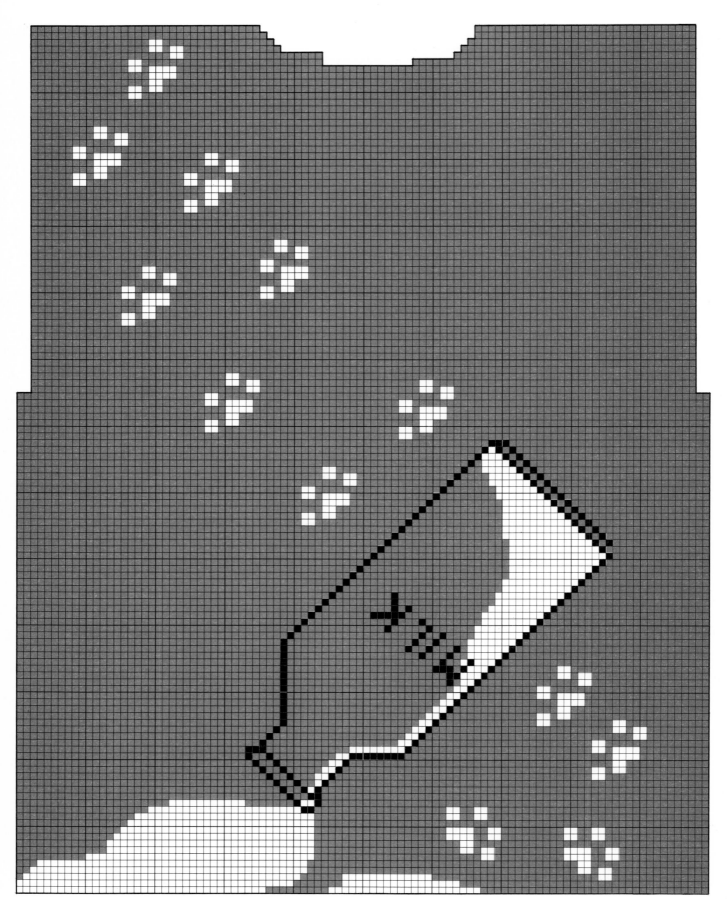

40

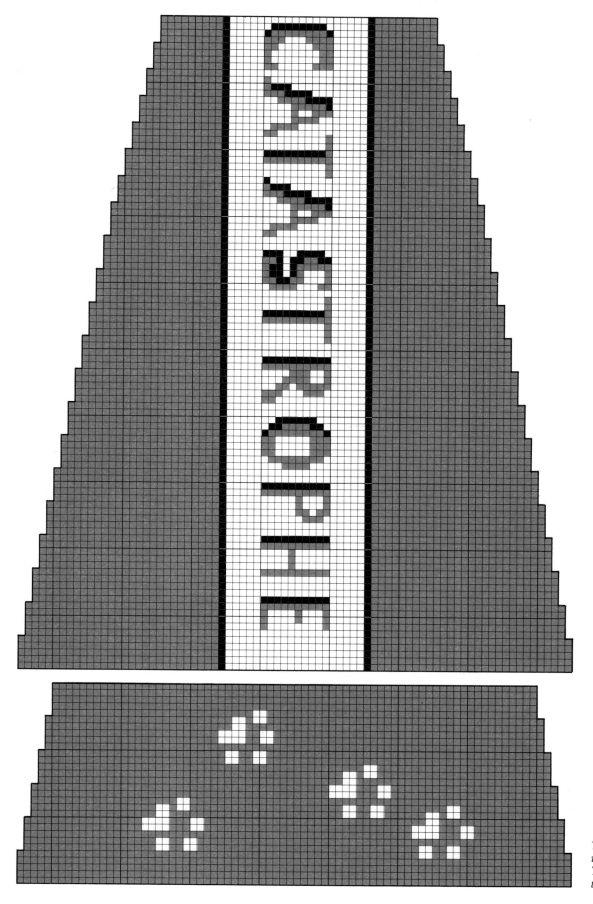

The graph opposite (page 40) is for the back of the sweater. The graph on this page shows the sleeve.

Right sleeve

Using 6mm needles and black, cast on 40 sts.

Row 1: *k2 black, p2 white to end. Row 2: k2 white, p2 black to end. Repeat these 2 rows until work measures 7cm.

Change to main colour* and cont following graph in stocking stitch, inc 1 st at each end of the 4th row and the 6 following 4th rows. Then inc 1 st at each end of the 13 following 5th rows (80 sts). Work 4 rows. Cast off.

Left sleeve

Work as for right sleeve to *. Change to main colour only and cont in stocking stitch, shaping as for right sleeve until you have 70 sts. Begin reading graph for left sleeve and cont shaping as shown until graph is complete. Cast off.

Neckband

With RS of work together, knit left shoulder seam (see Techniques, pages 15–16). Turn work back to RS and, with main colour and 5½mm needles, pick up and knit 72 sts evenly around neck to include those held on holders for back and front. K2, p2 rib for 6cm. Cast off. Knit right shoulder seams together, turn neckband inwards and slip stitch cast-off edge to pick-up edge.

Making up

Join sleeves to jumper; join sleeve and side seams with a flat seam.

PRISCILLA MOHAIR COAT

This curve-fronted mohair coat is worked entirely in stocking stitch using the intarsia method (*see* Techniques, pages 9–10).

Materials
Melinda Coss mohair – charcoal: 525gm; emerald: 100gm; jade, fuchsia and white: 50gm; cornflower, lemon, gold, purple, orange, black, coral, scarlet, silver and pink: less than 25gm of each.

Needles
One pair of 5½mm needles.

Tension
Using 5½mm needles and measured over st st, 16 sts and 16 rows = 10cm square.

Back
Using 5½mm needles and main colour, cast on 112 sts. Beginning with a knit row, follow graph for back in st st to beg of raglan shaping. Cast off 2 sts at beg of the next 2 rows, then dec 1 st at each end of every alt row until graph is complete. Cast off remaining 18 sts.

Right front
Using 5½mm needles and main colour, cast on 8 sts. Begin following the graph in st st, casting on 7 sts at end of the 2nd row. Work 2 rows, casting on 5 sts at end of the 2nd row and the following alt row. K 1 row, p 1 row, cast on 3 sts. K 1 row, p 1 row, cast on 2 sts. K 1 row, p back, inc once in the last st. Cont to inc 1 st at shaped edge on every row until you have 49 sts. Then inc 1 st at every alt row until you have 59 sts. Cont straight, without further shaping until 71 rows have been completed from beg of work.
Shape armholes: next row (WS): cast off 2 sts at beg of this row. Cast off 1 st at armhole edge on the next 8 alt rows (49 sts). Work 1 row. Cont to dec 1 st at armhole edge on every alt row. **Shape neck** by casting off 1 st at neck edge on next row and the 11 following 6th rows. Work straight at neck edge for 5 rows, while cont to shape sleeve edge until you have one stitch. Fasten off.

Left front
Work as for right front, but read left front graph and reverse shapings.

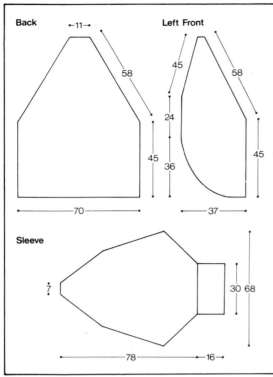

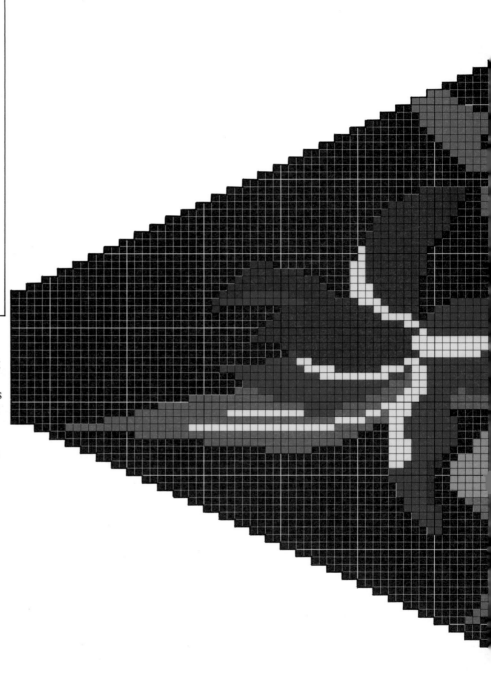

Sleeves
Using 5½mm needles and main colour, cast on 48 sts. Begin following the appropriate graph (pages 48–9), working the first 4 rows in garter stitch. Then work in k6, p6 rib for 22 rows, inc 5 sts evenly across last row of rib (53 sts). Cont following graph, working in st st and inc 1 st at each end of every row until you have 109 sts. Work 3 rows without shaping, then dec 1 st at each end of the next row and the 6 following 4th rows, then every alt row 27 times (41 sts), then at each end of every row until you have 11 sts. Cast off.

Collar (Knitted in one piece)
Using 5½mm needles, cast on 30 sts. Row 1: k6, p6, k6, p6, k6. Row 2: p6, k6, p6, k6, p6. Repeat these 2 rows until the border fits all around the outer edge of the coat, beginning and ending at the centre-back neck. Cast off.

Making up
Join raglan seams of back and sleeves, then join each front raglan to sleeves. Join side and sleeve seams using invisible seams throughout.

44

*The graph above shows the
back of the coat.*

45

The two graphs opposite are for the front of the coat – the one on the left of the page is for the right front, the one on the right is for the left front.

46

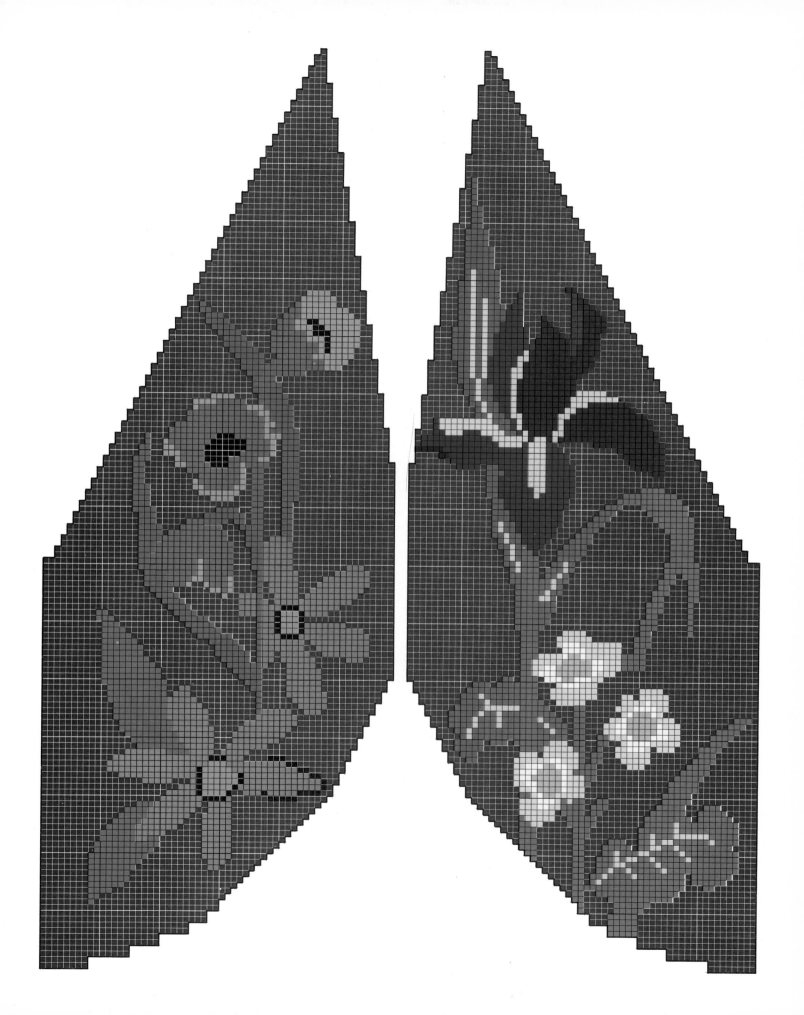

*Graph for the left sleeve of
the Priscilla Mohair Coat.*

48

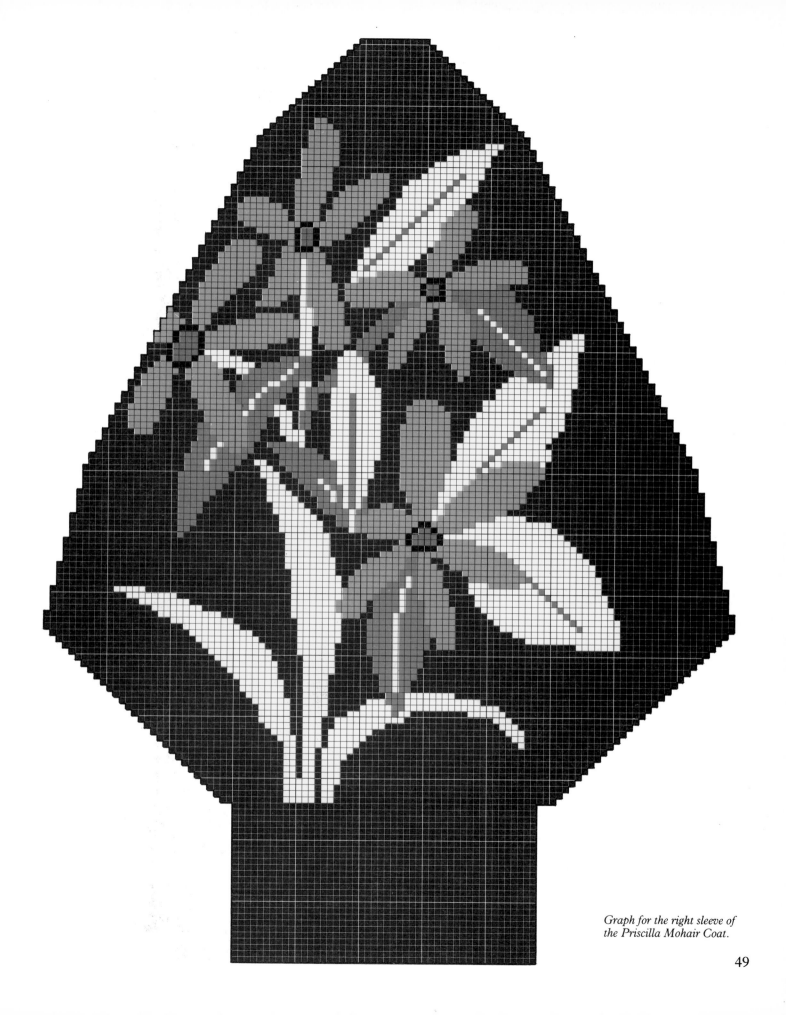

Graph for the right sleeve of the Priscilla Mohair Coat.

49

GINGYPOP TWEED RAGLAN JUMPER

Materials

Melinda Coss tweed – black heather: 700gm; Melinda Coss mohair – ginger, rust, chestnut, white, black, peach, orange, green and silver: 25gm of each; turquoise chenille: 50gm.

Needles

One pair of 4½mm and one pair of 5½mm needles; one 4½mm circular needle.

Tension

Using 5½mm needles and measured over st st, 16 sts and 24 rows = 10cm square. Ribs worked on 4½mm needles.

This simple-to-knit raglan jumper is worked mainly in stocking stitch using the intarsia method (*see* Techniques, pages 9–10).

Back

Using 4½mm needles and main colour, cast on 90 sts. Work in k2, p2 rib for 8cm, inc 12 sts evenly across the last row of rib (102 sts). Change to 5½mm needles and cont in st st for 10 rows, then begin reading goldfish graph as follows: k18 base, k first row of graph, k to end. This sets your position for the graph. Work until complete, then cont in main colour only until work measures 41cm, ending with an RS row.

Shape raglan: cast off 2 sts at beg of the next 2 rows. Purl 1 row. Next row: k3, sl 1, k1, psso, k to last 5 sts, k2 tog, k3. Repeat the last 2 rows until 26 sts remain.

Shape neck: p8, cast off 10 sts, p8. Slip

first set of 8 sts onto a holder and work on last set only. Dec 1 st at neck edge on next 4 rows. Work 3 rows without shaping. Cast off.

Front

Work as for back until 12 rows of st st have been completed. Next row (RS): k58 in main colour, k6 in turquoise, k40 in main colour. Cont working graph in this position until it is complete. *At the same time*, when work measures 41cm, commence shaping raglan as for back, then cont in main colour only. When 34 sts remain, **shape neck:** next row (WS): p12, cast off 10 sts, p to end. Cont with this set of sts, leaving others on a holder. Dec 1 st at neck edge on the next 4 rows. Meanwhile, cont raglan shaping as before. Now work the neck edge straight and cont shaping raglan until 2 sts remain. Work 2 rows straight. P2 tog, secure off. Return to other side of neck,

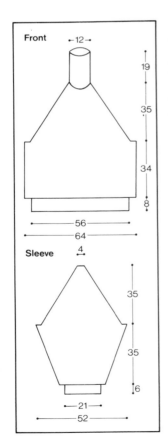

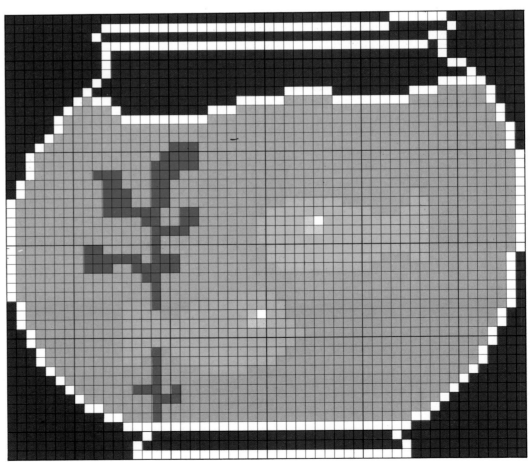

Goldfish graph for the back of the jumper.

50

joining in yarn at neck edge. Work to match first side.

Sleeves

Using main colour and 4½mm needles, cast on 36 sts, and work in k2, p2 rib for 6cm. Change to 5½mm needles and cont, in st st, inc 1 st at each end of every 3rd row until you have 90 sts. Work straight until the sleeve measures 41cm, ending with an RS row. **Shape raglan:** work as for back until 8 sts remain. Work 2 rows straight, then cast off. Work 2nd sleeve to match.

Collar

Join all raglans with a flat seam. Using a 4½mm circular needle and with RS facing, knit up 104 sts evenly around the neck. K 1 row, then cont in k2, p2 rib for 19cm. Cast off loosely in rib.

Tail

Using 5½mm needles, cast on 3 sts in ginger. Work in st st, increasing and decreasing as shown on graph. When tail is complete, fold in half lengthways and join the two long edges together with an invisible seam. Attach to jumper at top point where indicated with an 'X'.

Making up

Join all remaining seams using a flat seam.

The graph below is for the tail, which is attached to the front of the jumper.

The graph on page 52 shows the front of the jumper with the Gingypop design. If you want to add the finishing touches to Gingypop, the solid black lines indicate where you can embroider the mouth and claws. 'X' shows where the tail should be attached.

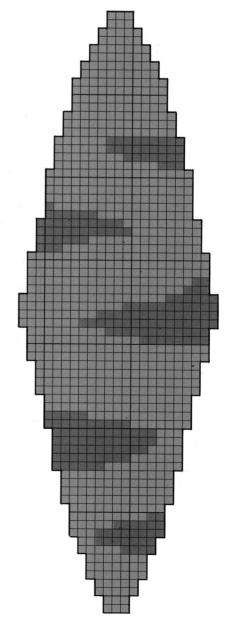

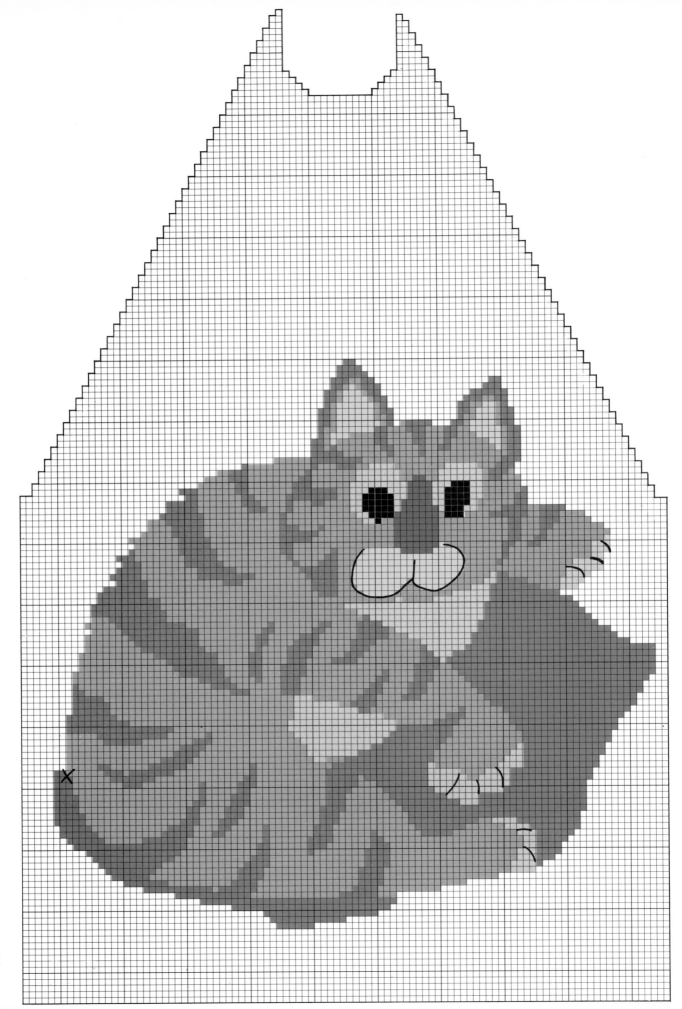

52

KITTY TRACKSUIT

Materials

Melinda Coss DK wool – emerald: 650/700/750gm; silver-grey, black, white, ginger, pink and blue: less than 50gm of each.

Needles

One pair of 3½mm and one pair of 4mm needles.

Tension

Using 4mm needles and measured over st st, 23 sts and 30 rows = 10cm square. Ribs worked on 3½mm needles.

A snug tracksuit for 8/10/12-year-olds using double-knitting wool and worked in stocking stitch using the intarsia method (*see* Techniques, pages 9–10). A special pocket is included for the safe-keeping of mittens.

Front

Using 3½mm needles, cast on 90/94/102 sts and work 7/7/7cm in k2, p2 rib, inc 1/3/1 st evenly across last row of rib (91/97/103 sts). Change to 4mm needles and begin in st st for 8/10/12 rows. Next row (RS): begin working graph 1, positioning as follows: k12/15/18 sts. Work first row of graph 1, k to end. This sets the position for the first graph. Work until it is complete. Work 12/16/20 rows in main colour only. Begin graph 2, placing as follows: k38/41/44 sts. Work first row of graph 2, k to end. Cont following this graph in position as set until 38 rows have been completed.

Shape raglan: size 1: cast off 3 sts at beg of the next 2 rows, then cast off 2 sts at beg of the next 6 rows. Cast off 1 st at each end of the next 24 alt rows.

Size 2: cast off 3 sts at beg of the next 2 rows. Cast off 2 sts at beg of the next 6 rows. Cast off 1 st at each end of the next 26 rows.

Size 3: cast off 2 sts at beg of the next 10 rows. Cast off 1 st at each end of the next 28

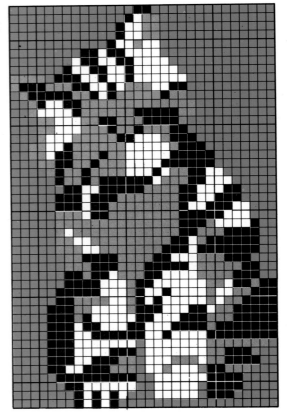

alt rows. *At the same time*, when work measures 43/47/50cm from the start, **shape neck:** cast off centre 13 sts and, working

Graph 1 is for the tabby cat on the front of the top.

Graph 2 is the black and white cat.

Start both graphs at the bottom right hand corner.

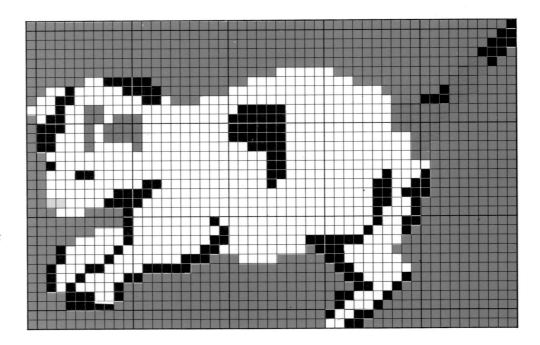

54

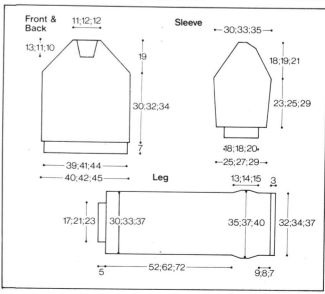

Front & Back

11;12;12

13;11;10

19

30;32;34

7

←39;41;44→

←40;42;45→

Sleeve

←30;33;35→

18;19;21

23;25;29

18;18;20

←25;27;29→

Leg

13;14;15   3

17;21;23   30;33;37   35;37;40   32;34;37

5   ←52;62;72→   9;8;7

55

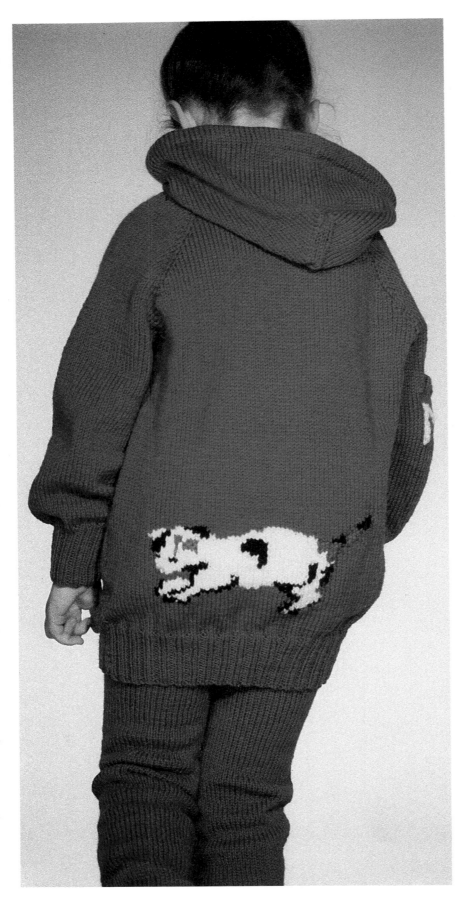

each side separately, cast off 3 sts at neck edge on the next 2 alt rows, then cast off 2 sts on the next alt row and then cast off 1 st at neck edge on the next alt row/the next 2 alt rows/the next 2 alt rows. Cast off remaining 2 sts.

Back

Work as for front until the first 10 rows of st st have been completed. Row 11: k26. K first row of graph 3, k to end. Cont as for back, working graph 3 in position as set until it is complete. Cont as for front in main colour only, but ignore neck shaping. When raglans are complete, cast off remaining 25/27/27sts.

Pocket-lining

Using 4mm needles and main colour, cast on 50 sts. Work in st st for 45 rows. Leave these sts on a spare needle.

Right sleeve

Using 3½mm needles and main colour, cast on 42/42/46 sts. Work in k2, p2 rib for 24 rows, inc 16/20/20 sts evenly across last row of rib (58/62/66 sts). Cont working in st st, inc 1 st at each end of every 10th row 6/7/7 times. *At the same time*, when 48 rows have been completed, begin graph 4, positioning as follows: k7/9/11 sts. K first row of graph 4. K to end. Cont working graph in this position (inc every 10th row as set) until graph is complete. Work 4 rows in main colour only. **Make pocket opening:** k8. Slip the next 50 sts onto a holder, rejoin yarn, k to end. Purl back, replacing held sts with sts from pocket-lining. Cont in main colour only until the sleeve measures 31/33/37cm, ending with a purl row. **Shape armhole:** cast off 2 sts at beg of the next 2 rows. Cast off 1 st at beg of the next 44/48/52 rows. While cont to dec 1 st at beg of every purl row, dec 4 sts at beg of the next 3/3/3 knit rows. (Sizes 2 and 3 only: then dec 3 sts at beg of the next knit row.) Cont to dec 1 st at beg of every purl row only until 5 sts remain. Work 1 row. Cast off.

Left sleeve

Work as for right sleeve, reversing shapings and omitting pocket.

HOOD

Using 4mm needles, cast on 132/142/142 sts and work in st st for 7/8/8cm. *Next row

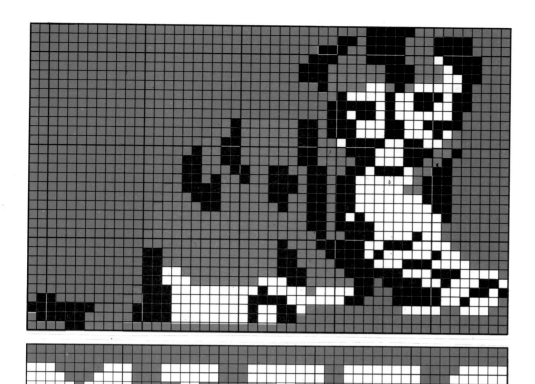

Start graphs at bottom right hand corner.

Graph 3 should be incorporated into the back.

Graph 4 should be incorporated into the right sleeve.

(RS): k128/138/138 sts, turn, p124/134/134 sts, turn, then work 6 rows across all sts.★ Rep from ★ to ★ 6 times more. *At the same time,* when work measures 15/16/16cm, dec 1 st at each side of the 2 centre sts on every alt row 15 times – i.e., k63/68/68 sts, k2 tog, k2, k2 tog, k63/63/68. Next row: p62/67/67, p2 tog, p2, p2 tog. P62/67/67, etc. Cast off remaining sts. Join back seam of hood, then, using slip stitch, make a 2cm hem on outer edge of hood.

Making up
Sew sleeve pocket-lining into position.
Pocket welt: using 3½mm needles and main colour, pick up the 50 sts held for pocket and work in k2, p2 rib for 4 rows, cast off. Join raglans with an invisible seam and join side and sleeve seams. Join hood to neck edge.

TROUSERS

Legs (Both alike)
Using 3½mm needles, cast on 40/48/54 sts. Work in k2, p2 rib for 5cm, inc 30 sts evenly across last row of rib (70/76/84 sts). Change to 4mm needles and work straight until leg measures 52/62/72cm. Inc 1 st at each end of the next row and the 4 following 3rd/4th/5th rows. Work 4 rows without shaping, then dec 1 st at each end of the next row and the 4 following 5th rows. Work without shaping until leg measures 74/84/94cm from beg. Change back to 3½mm needles and work in k2, p2 rib for 3cm. Cast off.

Making up
Join leg seams together with an invisible seam. Join rise. Turn waist hem inwards and slip stitch down, leaving an opening for elastic. Thread an appropriate length of elastic through the opening and oversew. Join opening.

CAT WITH SARDINES SWEATER

Materials
Melinda Coss tussah silk – ecru: 550gm; jade: 250gm. Angora – black: 30gm; chocolate, rose and white: less than 20gm of each. Mohair – rust: 25gm. DK wool – ginger, emerald, gold, cornflower and slate: less than 50gm of each. Silver lurex ribbon: less than 50gm.

Needles
One pair of 3¼mm and one pair of 4mm needles; one pair of 3¼mm double-pointed needles.

Tension
Using 4mm needles and measured over st st, 22 sts and 30 rows = 10cm square. Ribs worked on 3¼mm needles.

A luxury silk and angora sweater worked using the intarsia method (*see* Techniques, pages 9–10).

The graph opposite shows the front of the sweater. Solid black lines show where to embroider the eyes, mouth and writing on the tin.

58

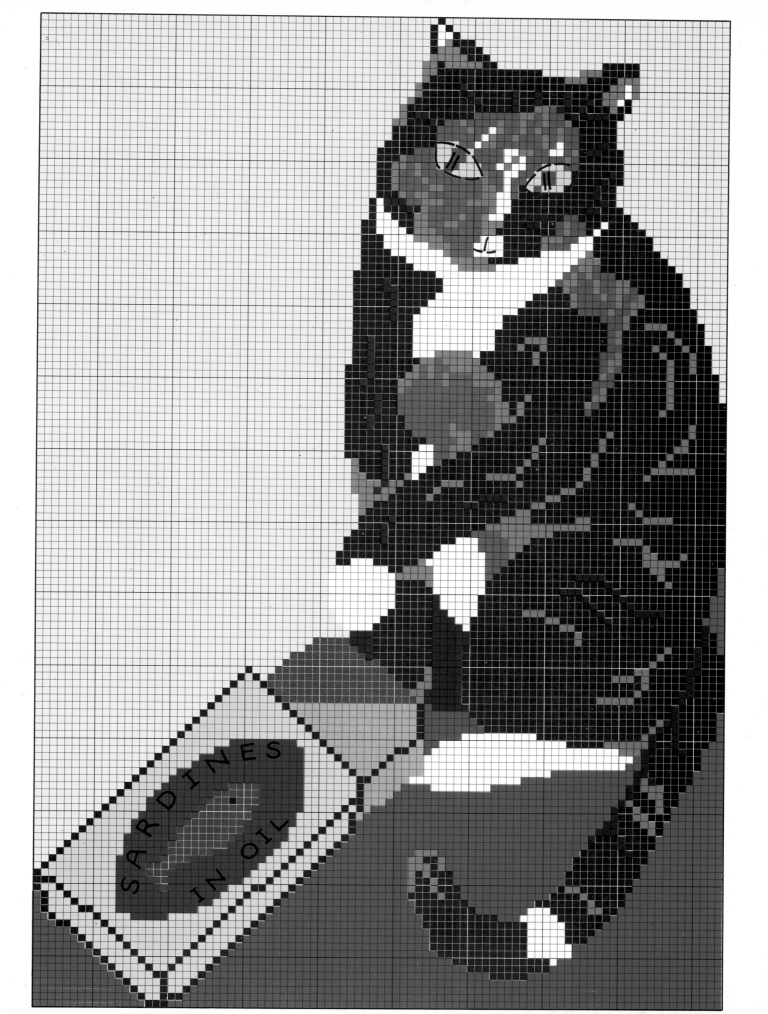

Front

Using 3¼mm needles, cast on 118 sts in jade. K1, p1 rib for 7cm. Change to 4mm needles and begin in st st, inc 1 st at the end of the first row (119 sts). Work in st st in jade only for 24 rows, then commence following graph positioning as follows. First row: k14, k first row of graph, k13. When 41 rows of the graph have been worked, make slit for sardine tin as follows: next row (WS): p46, p18, slip the last 18 sts onto a holder, p to end. On return row, still following the graph, cast on 18 sts over those held. Cont following the graph until it is complete. St st 20 rows in ecru.

Shape neck (RS): row 1: k44, turn and cont on these sts only. Row 2: p2, p2 tog, p to end, turn. Row 3: k to last 4 sts, k2 tog, k2. Rep these last 2 rows until 37 sts remain. St st 4 rows, leave sts on a holder for the shoulder. Slip the centre 31 sts onto a holder, rejoin yarn to remaining sts and work dec rows as follows: Row 1: p to last 4 sts, p2 tog tbl, p2. Row 2: k2, ssk, k to end of row. Repeat these last 2 rows until 37 sts remain. Work 4 rows in ecru only and slip these sts onto a spare needle.

Back

Using 3¼mm needles and jade, cast on 118 sts and work in k1, p1 rib for 7cm. Change to 4mm needles and increase 1 st at the end of the first row (119 sts). Work in st st in jade only for 14 rows. Next row (RS): k9, k first row of graph, k to end. This sets your position for the graph work in st st until it is complete. When row 86 has been worked, change to ecru and cont in st st until back matches front to neck shaping. Shape neck as for front, leaving shoulder sts on a spare needle. Place front and back RS together and knit shoulder seams together (*see* Techniques, pages 15–16).

Sleeves

Using 3¼mm needles and ecru, cast on 46 sts. K1, p1 rib for 9cm, inc 13 sts evenly across last row of rib (59 sts). Change to 4mm needles and work in st st, inc 1 st at each end of the 2nd row and every following 4th row until you have 127 sts. Cast off loosely.

Neckband

Using 3¼mm double-pointed needles and ecru, pick up and knit 110 sts evenly around the neck. K1, p1 rib for 7 rows.

Cast off in rib.

Sardine tin

Using 4mm needles (RS facing) and silver lurex, pick up the 18 sts held for sardine tin. Work in st st, dec 1 st at each end of every row until you have 2 sts. K2 tog, fasten off. Leave this triangle to roll back on itself.

Fish (Make 2)

Using 4mm needles and silver lurex, cast on 2 sts. Work in garter st, inc 1 st at each end of every row until you have 8 sts. Work 5 rows straight, dec 1 st at each end of every row until you have 4 sts, then inc 1 st at each end of the next 3 rows. Work 2 rows straight, dec 1 st at each end of the next 3 rows (4 sts). Inc 1 st at each end of the next 2 rows. Work 5 rows straight, dec 1 st at each end of every row until 1 st remains. Fasten off. Fold fish in half and join side seams together. Embroider eye and mouth as indicated in photograph.

Making up

Using silver lurex, slot fish tails into position as shown on photograph and sew along opening. Tack fish heads into position on cat's paw. Embroider as indicated on graph using backstitch. Join sleeves to jumper and join sleeve and side seams.

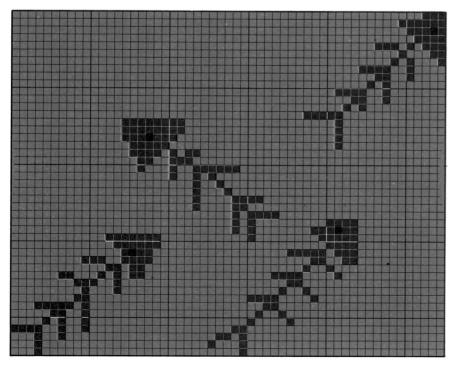

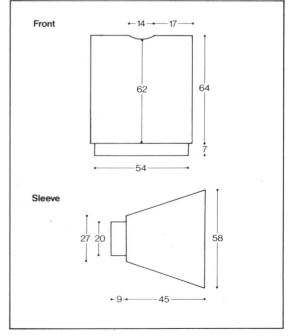

Graph for sardines on the back of the sweater.

CAT BURGLAR JUMPER

Materials
Melinda Coss DK
mercerized cotton: olive:
500gm; black: 50gm;
white: 100gm; oddments
of gold and bright green.

Needles
One pair of 3¼mm and
one pair of 4mm needles.

Tension
Using 4mm needles and
measured over st st, 22
sts and 26 rows = 10cm
square. Ribs worked on
3¼mm needles.

This cropped double-knitting cotton jumper is simple to make using the intarsia method (*see* Techniques, pages 9–10).

The graph opposite is for the front of the jumper.

The graph for the back of the jumper is on page 64.

The graph for the sleeve is on page 66.

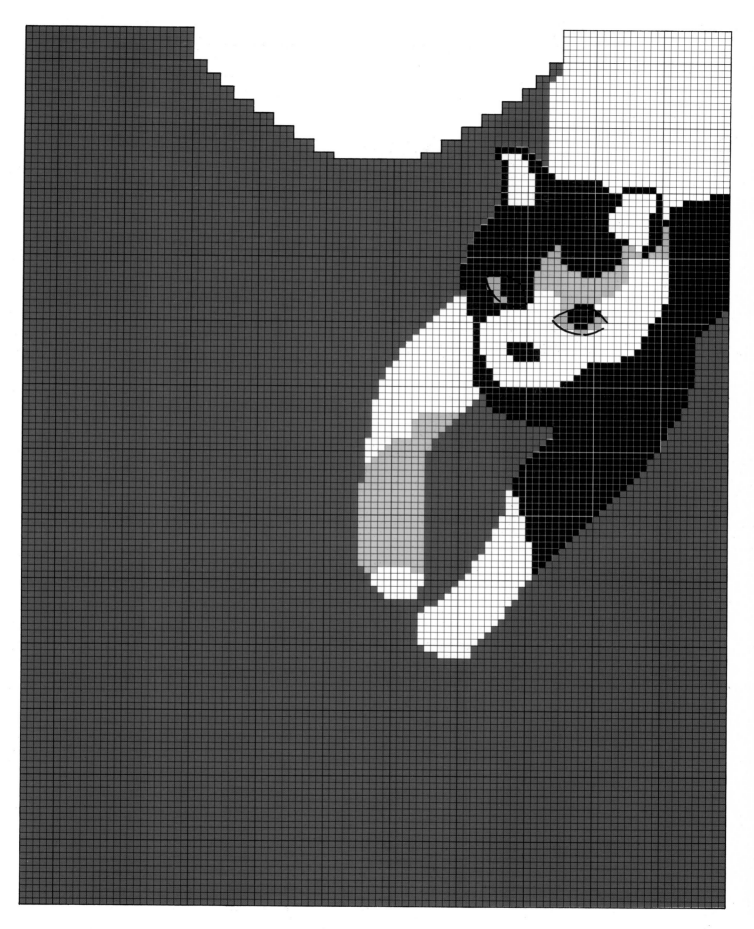

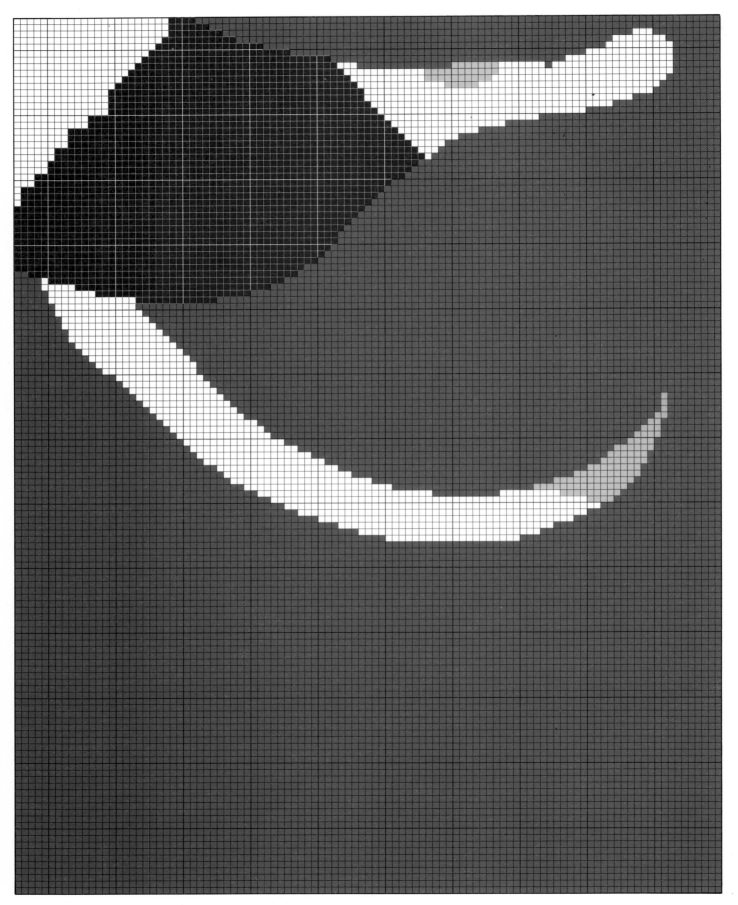

64

Back

Using 3¼mm needles and main colour, cast on 104 sts. K2, p2 rib for 10 rows, inc 1 st at beg of the last row of rib (105 sts). ★ Change to 4mm needles and, commencing with a knit row, work without shaping in st st for 134 rows, following the graph for the back. Cast off 25 sts at beg of the next 2 rows. Leave centre 55 sts on a spare needle.

Pocket-lining

Using 4mm needles and main colour, cast on 28 sts. Work in st st for 30 rows. Leave these sts on a holder.

Front

Work as for back to ★. Change to 4mm needles and, beginning with a knit row, st st, following the graph for front until 30 rows (excluding rib) have been completed. Next row: **make pocket**: k65. Slip next 28 sts onto a holder. K12 to end. Return row: p12. P28 sts from pocket-lining, p65 to end. Cont following the graph to row 114.

Shape neck: k46. Slip remaining 59 sts onto a spare needle and work on first set of 46 sts only. Turn. Cast off 3 sts at beg of the next row and the 4 following alt rows, then cast off 2 sts at beg of the next 3 alt rows. Work 5 rows without shaping. Cast off remaining 25 sts. Return to the 59 sts held and slip centre 13 sts onto a stitch holder. Rejoin yarn and shape as for other side of neck, reversing shapings.

Left sleeve

Using 3¼mm needles and main colour, cast on 38 sts and work in k2, p2 rib for 10 rows. Change to 4mm needles and commence following sleeve graph in st st, inc 1 st at each end of every 3rd row until you have 108 sts. Work 2 rows. Cast off loosely.

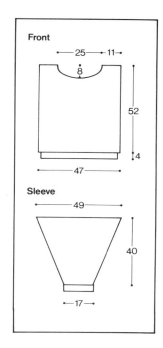

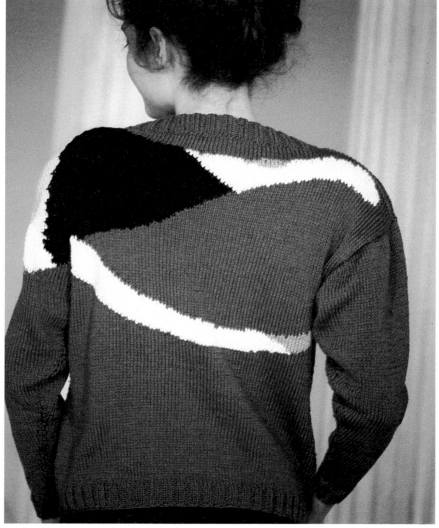

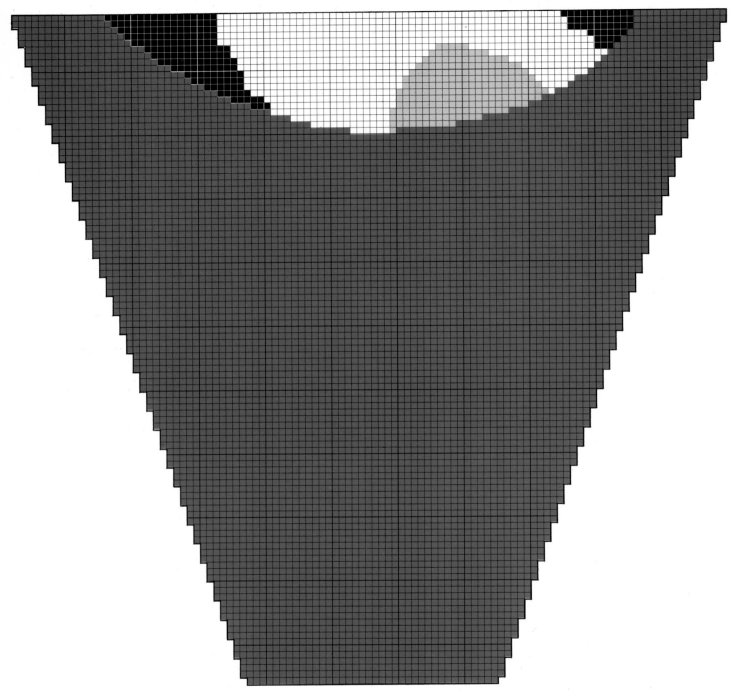

Right sleeve
Work as for left sleeve, but use main colour only.

Neckband
Join right shoulder seam using a flat seam. Using 3¼mm needles, pick up and knit 23 sts down left neck, 13 sts held for centre front, 23 sts up right neck, 55 sts across back. Work in k2, p2 rib for 20 rows. Cast off. Join other shoulder seam. Turn neckband inwards and slip stitch cast-off edge to pick-up edge.

Pocket welt
Using 3¼mm needles and main colour, pick up the 28 sts held for pocket top and k1, p1 rib for 4 rows. Cast off. Stitch pocket-lining and welt into position.

Making up
Join sleeves to jumper using narrow backstitch and taking care to match design on left sleeve to front. Join sleeve and side seams using a flat seam. Embroider eyes as indicated (*see* Techniques, page 17).

SIAMESE CAT DRESS

This slinky dress with button-through back is simple to knit. The pattern is shown in two sizes and is worked using the intarsia method (*see* Techniques, pages 9–10).

Materials
Melinda Coss satin
ribbon – black: 800gm;
silver lurex: 50gm. 12
buttons.

Needles
One pair of 4½mm, one
pair of 5mm and one pair
of 5½mm needles.

Tension
Using 5½mm needles
and measured over st st,
22 sts and 28 rows =
10cm square.

Front

Using 5mm needles and main colour, cast
on 103/109 sts.
Row 1: p1, *k1, p1, rep from * to end.
Row 2: k1, *p1, k1, rep from * to end.
Repeat the last 2 rows 3 times.
　　Change to 5½mm needles and work 2/10
rows in st st, using main colour only.
Commence the cat motif, placing as
indicated on the graph. Cont following the
graph until 144/148 rows have been worked
(excluding rib). Cast off 1 st at each end of
the next row and the following 12/13 alt
rows. Cont without further shaping until
row 196/204. Inc 1 st at each end of the next
row and the following 9 alt rows (97/101 sts).
Work without shaping for another 40 rows.
Shape neck: k40/42 sts. Slip remaining
57/59 sts on to a spare needle. Turn and,
working on first set of sts only, cast off 3 sts
at beg of this row and the next alt row,

keeping armhole edge straight. Cont
straight at armhole edge, cast off 2 sts at
beg of the next alt row, then 1 st at neck
edge on every row until you have 24/26 sts.
Work 4 rows straight, leave remaining sts
on a spare needle. Return to the 57/59 sts
held on a spare needle and place centre 17
sts on a stitch holder, rejoin yarn to
remaining 40/42 sts and work to match left
side of neck, reversing shapings.

Left back

Using 5mm needles and main colour, cast
on 57/59 sts and work rib as for front, but
on last row inc 0/1 sts mid-row (57/60 sts).
Slip first 8 sts onto a safety-pin for back
band. Work in st st until back matches
front to start of shaping, ending with a knit
row (the work should measure approxi-
mately 54/55 cm). Cast off 1 st at beg of the
next and every alt row until you have 36/38

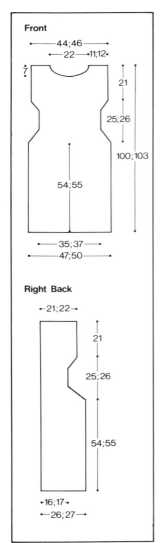

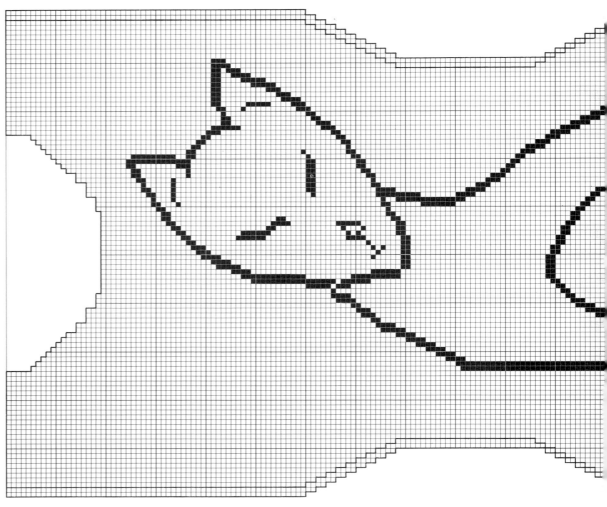

sts. Work straight for 28/30 rows, ending with a knit row. Inc 1 st at beg of the next and every alt row until you have 46/48 sts. Work without further shaping until back matches front in length. Leave sts on a spare needle.

Right back

Work rib as for left back. Slip last 8 sts on to a safety-pin for back band. Cont to match left back, reversing shapings. When work matches front and left back, leave sts on a spare needle.

Shoulder seams

With RS of work facing, take the first 24/26 sts from one shoulder and knit these together with the sts from corresponding front shoulder (*see* Techniques, pages 15–16). Leave remaining sts on a spare needle. Repeat for other side.

Buttonband

Slip the 8 sts held on a safety-pin from left back on to a 5mm needle. Using main colour, k1, p1 rib these sts until the band fits up the back to neck when slightly stretched. Break off yarn and leave sts on a safety-pin. Sew band on to back piece. Mark 12 button positions up the band, the first button to be placed 14/17cm from cast-on edge, the last one 7cm below safety-pin and the remaining 10 spaced equally (approx every 7cm).

Buttonhole band

Work as for buttonband, working buttonholes when markers reached as follows: 1st row: rib 3, cast off 2 sts, rib 3; return row: rib 3, cast on 2 sts, rib 3.

Collar

With RS of work facing and using 4½mm

The design for the Siamese cat on the front of the dress is shown in the graph below. Note that the graph has been reproduced horizontally but should be knitted vertically from tail to head. The inner outline is for the smaller size.

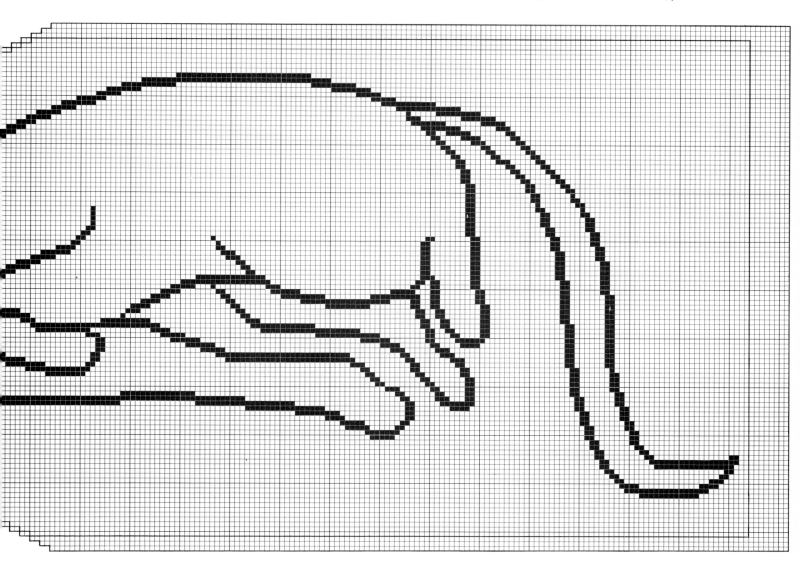

needles and main colour, rib across 8 sts, from buttonband, 22 sts from back, 24 sts down left front, 8 sts across front to middle st (k2 into next st). Rib 8 sts across front, 24 sts up right front, 22 sts from back and 8 sts across band (126 sts). Next row: work one buttonhole as described before. Rib to end. Cont in rib for 5cm. Work another buttonhole, rib 4 rows. Cast off in rib.

Armhole bands

Place a pin 21/22cm down from shoulder seam on back and front. With 5mm needles and main colour, pick up and knit 88/94 sts in between markers. Work in k1, p1 rib for 3cm. Cast off in rib.

Making up

Sew in all ends *securely*. Join side seams using a narrow backstitch. Sew on buttons.

'MEOW' FAIRISLE SWEATER

Materials
Melinda Coss 4-ply wool – black: 275gm; ecru: 125gm; grey: 100gm; rust and sky blue: 50gm; green, beige, amber and yellow: 25gm.

Needles
One pair of 2¾mm and one pair of 3¼mm needles.

Tension
Using 3¼mm needles and measured over fairisle pattern, 28 sts and 28 rows = 10cm square. Ribs worked on 2¾mm needles.

This drop-shoulder sweater in 4-ply wool uses the fairisle technique of colour knitting (*see* Techniques, pages 8–9).

Back
Using 2¾mm needles and black, cast on 150 sts. K1, p1 rib for 7cm, inc 4 sts evenly across the last row. Change to 3¼mm needles and work 2 rows in st st, starting with a knit row. Begin following graph 1 as follows: work 3 repeats across the row plus 4 sts. Work as set until the 6 rows are complete. Now work 4 rows in main colour only. Graph 2: k2 in main colour, k first row of graph, working 3 repeats in all, k4 in main colour . Work as set until the graph is complete. Work 4 rows in main colour. Graph 3: k first row of graph, working 3 repeats in all plus 4 sts. Work as set until the 6 rows are complete. Work 4 rows in main colour. Graph 4: work as for graph 2. Work 4 rows in main colour. Work graph 5 as for graph 1. Work 4 rows in main colour, then work graph 6 (3 repeats). Rep from beg until graph 3 is complete, work 4 rows in main colour, then rep graph 6. Work 7 rows in main colour. Leave sts on a spare needle.

Front
Work as for back until graph 2 has been repeated. Work 4 rows in main colour, then follow graph 3.
Shape neck: work 66 sts. Cast off 22 sts, work to end. Cont with this set of sts, keeping in pattern as for back and leaving other sts on a holder. Dec 1 st at neck edge on every row until 46 sts remain. Now work straight until the front matches the back. Leave sts on a holder. Return to other set of

sts. Join in yarn at neck edge and shape to match first side. Leave sts on a holder.

Sleeves
Using 2¾mm needles and black, cast on 56 sts and work in k1, p1 rib for 10cm, ending with an RS row and inc 18 sts evenly across last row of rib (74 sts). Change to 3¼mm needles and start working the graphs and main colour rows until graphs 1–6 are complete. Work 4 rows in main colour, rep graph 1. Work 4 rows in main colour, rep graph 6. Work 2 rows in main colour. *At the same time*, inc 1 st at each end of every 4th row until you have 124 sts (working all new sts into colour pattern as you go). Now inc 1 st at each end of every 3rd row until you have 140 sts. Cast off loosely.

Neckband
Knit the left shoulder seam together (RS facing) and, using 2¾mm needles, slip the 62 back neck sts onto one needle. With RS of work facing, pick up 120 sts evenly around the neck. Purl 1 row, then work in k1, p1 rib for 3cm. Cast off loosely in rib.

Making up
Knit right shoulder seam together and join neckband with a flat seam. Join sleeves to jumper with a narrow backstitch, join side and sleeve seams with a flat seam. Press lightly using a damp cloth.

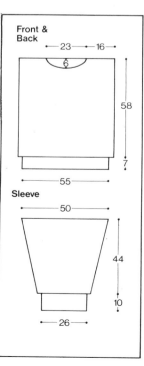

Front &
Back

|←—23—→|←—16—→|

6

58

7

55

Sleeve

50

44

10

26

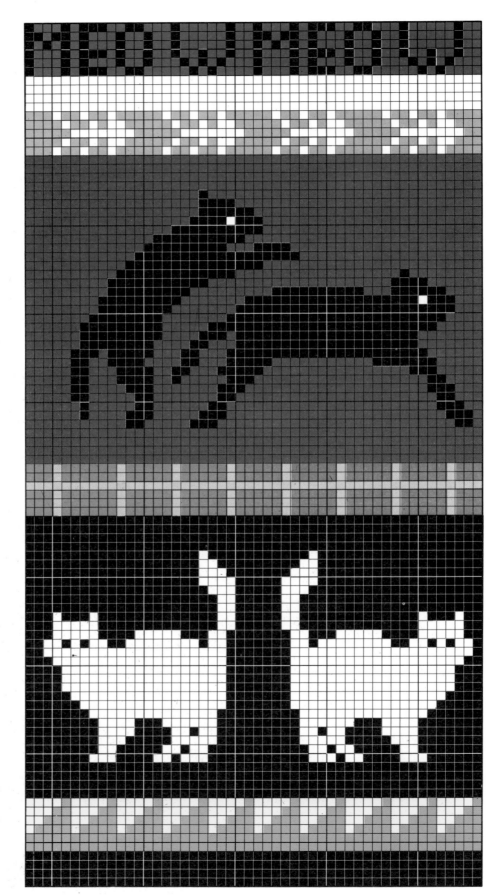

Graphs 1–6 for the "Meow" sweater. Graph 1 is the bottom, green pattern, graph 2 is the white cats, graph 3 the brown pattern, graph 4 the black cats, graph 5 the yellow pattern and graph 6 the word 'meow'.

CAT LOVE-LACE SWEATER

Materials
Melinda Coss 4-ply mercerized cotton — white 450gm; Melinda Coss angora – pink, caramel, chocolate, silver, slate and black: less than 20gm of each.

Needles
One pair of 2¾mm and one pair of 3¼mm needles; one 2¾mm circular needle.

Tension
Using 3¼mm needles and measured over st st, 28 sts and 36 rows = 10cm square.

N.B. Reading the graph: where no alternative instructions are given, the sweater should be worked in st st. The kittens are worked, using the colours given, in intarsia (*see* Techniques, pages 9–10) and the positioning of the lace panels are shown by a square inside the main square – for example, square 4 is worked in cable and ladder stitch. There are three repeats across the row and the square ends on a row 3 of the pattern. Stitches outside the inner square should be worked in st st.

A delicate sweater featuring panels of lace and pretty angora kittens. Worked in fine cotton, this is a project for the experienced knitter.

STITCH PANELS

Cable and ladder
Row 1 (WS and all other WS rows): k1, *p2 tog, yo, p11, k1; rep from *.
Row 2: k1, *ssk, yo, sl next 3 sts on to a cable needle and hold in back, k3, then k3 from cable needle, k6; rep from *.
Row 4: k1, *ssk, yo, k12, rep from *.
Row 6: k1, *ssk, yo, k3, sl next 3 sts on to a cable needle and hold in front, k3, then k3 from cable needle; k3, rep from *.
Row 8: rep row 4.

Lily of the valley
N.B. Make knot (MK) as follows: (k1, p1, k1, p1, k1) all in the same st, making 5 sts from 1, then pass the 4th, 3rd, 2nd and 1st of the new sts separately over the last st made.
Row 1 (WS and all other WS rows): k2, p23, k2.
Row 2 : p2, ssk, k6, (yo, k1) twice, sl 1, k2 tog, psso, (k1, yo) twice, k6, k2 tog, p2.
Row 4 : p2, ssk, k5, yo, k1, yo, k2, sl 1, k2 tog, psso, k2, yo, k1, yo, k5, k2 tog, p2.
Row 6 : p2, ssk, k4, yo, k1, yo, MK, k2, sl 1, k2 tog, psso, k2, MK, yo, k1, yo, k4, k2 tog, p2.
Row 8 : p2, ssk, k3, yo, k1, yo, MK, k3, sl 1, k2 tog, psso, k3, MK, yo, k1, yo, k3, k2 tog, p2.
Row 10: p2, ssk, k2, yo, k1, yo, MK, k4, sl 1, k2 tog, psso, k4, MK, yo, k1, yo, k2, k2 tog, p2.
Row 12: p2, ssk, (k1, yo) twice, MK, k5, sl 1, k2 tog, psso, k5, MK, (yo, k1) twice, k2 tog, p2.
Row 14: p2, ssk, yo, k1, yo, MK, k6, sl 1, k2 tog, psso, k6, MK, yo, k1, yo, k2 tog, p2.

Heart motif
N.B. $ = p1 st , return st to left-hand needle, keeping yarn in front, then pass *next* st over and off needle, then sl st back on to right-hand needle.

 # = p2 tog, return st to left-hand needle, keeping yarn in front, then pass *next* st over and off needle, then sl st back on to right-hand needle.

Row 1 and every alternate row: purl.
Row 2: knit.
Row 4: k12, yo, $, k11.
Row 6: k10, p2 tog, yo, k1B, yo, $, k10.
Row 8: k9, p2 tog, yo, k1B, yo, $, yo $, k9.
Row 10: k8, (p2 tog, yo) twice, k1B, (yo, $) twice k8.
Row 12: k7, (p2 tog, yo) twice, k18, yo, ($, yo), twice, $, k7.
Row 14: k6, (p2 tog, yo) 3 times, k1B, (yo, $) 3 times, k6.
Row 16: k5, (p2 tog, yo) 3 times, K1B, (yo, $) 4 times, k5.
Row 18: k4, (p2 tog, yo) 4 times, K1B, (yo, $) 4 times, k4.
Row 20: k3, (p2 tog, yo) 4 times, K1B, (yo, $) 5 times, k3.
Row 22: k2, (p2 tog, yo) 3 times, K1B, yo, $, yo, #, yo, p2 tog, yo, K1B, (yo, $) 3 times, k2.
Row 24: k1, (p2 tog, yo) 3 times, K1B, yo, $, yo, #, (yo, p2 tog) twice, yo, k1B, (yo, $) 3 times, k1.
Row 26: (p2 tog, yo) 3 times, K1B, (yo, $) twice, yo, #, yo, (p2 tog, yo) twice, K1B, (yo, $) 3 times.
Row 28: k1, yo, (p2 tog, yo) twice, #, yo, ($) twice, yo K1B, yo, (p2 tog, yo) twice, #, yo, ($, yo) twice, k1.
Row 30: ($, yo) 3 times, K1B, (yo, p2 tog) twice, yo, K1B, yo, ($) twice, yo, K1B, (yo, p2 tog) 3 times.
Row 32: k1, inc 1, yo, $, yo, * p2 tog, p3 tog tbl, pass the p2 tog st, over the p3 tog st, * yo, p2 tog, yo, inc 1, k1, inc 1, yo, $, yo, rep from * to *, yo, p2 tog, yo, inc 1, k1.

Front
Using 2¾mm needles and main colour, cast on 126 sts. Work in k1, p1 rib for 10cm, inc 11 sts evenly across last row of rib. Change to 3¼mm needles and begin following graph, reading each square as indicated on graph. **N.B.** Where an 'X' symbol appears on graph, make a bobble (MB) (*see* Techniques, page 11). Work the front, following the graph to armhole shaping. Cast off 5 sts at beg of the

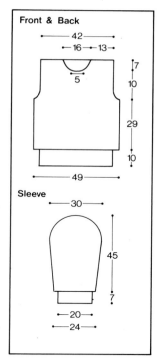

Front & Back

42
16 — 13
5
7
10
29
10
49

Sleeve

30
45
7
20
24

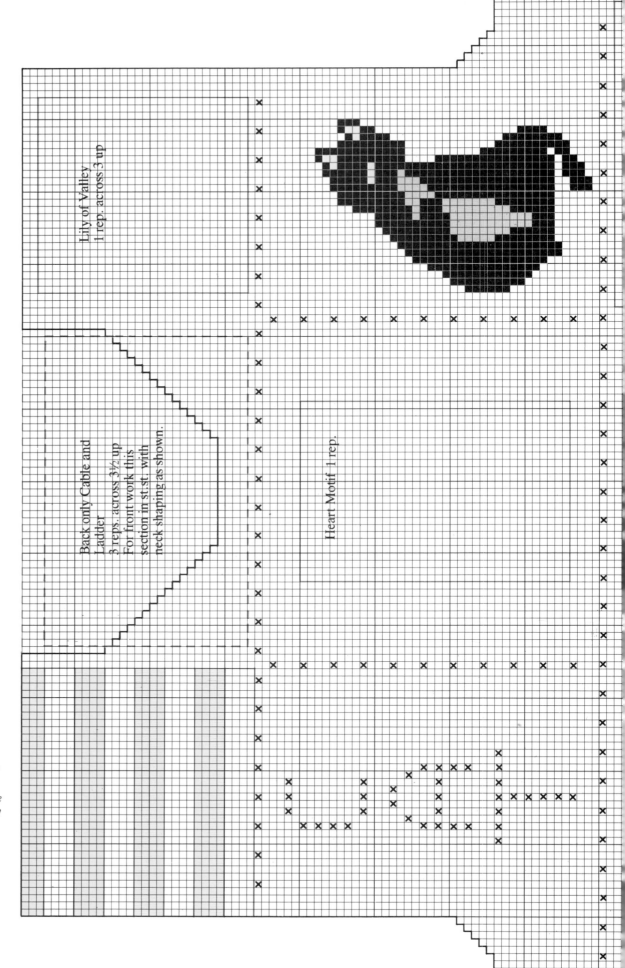

Graph for front and back of the Love-lace sweater. The solid blue line shows the edge of the back pattern. The lacy designs are inside the solid red lines. Where there is an 'x' on the graph, make a bobble. Note that the graph has been reproduced horizontally but you should knit it vertically from the right.

Lily of Valley
1 rep. across 3 up

Back only Cable and Ladder
3 reps. across 3½ up
For front work this section in st.st. with neck shaping as shown.

Heart Motif 1 rep.

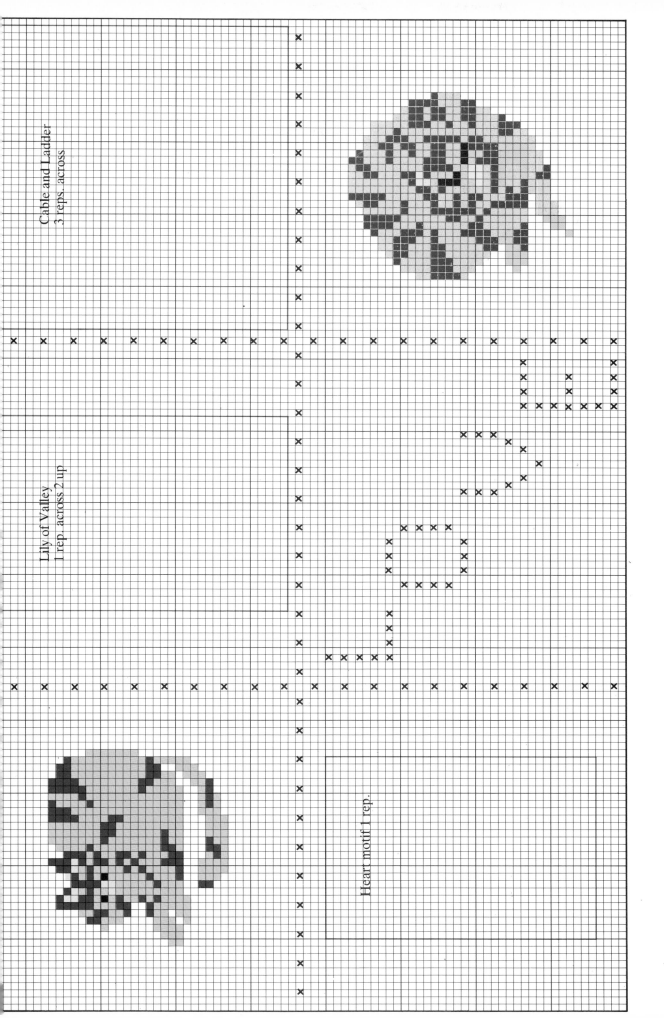

Cable and Ladder
3 reps. across

Lily of Valley
1 rep. across 2 up

Heart motif 1 rep.

77

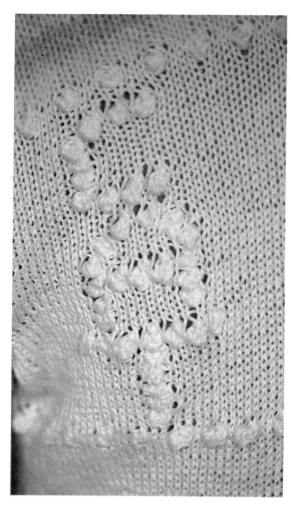

next 2 rows, then cast off 1 st at each end of the next 5 rows (117 sts). Work straight to **neck shaping**.

Next row: work 51 sts (leave the rest of the sts on a spare needle and work on this first set only). Dec 1 st at neck edge on the next 15 rows. Work 11 rows without shaping. Cast off. Rejoin yarn to held sts. Cast off centre 15 sts, knit to end. Repeat shaping as for other side.

Back

Work as for front, omitting the neck shaping and working central back square in cable and ladder as indicated.

Sleeves

Using 2¾mm needles, cast on 57 sts and work in k1, p1 rib for 7cm, inc 10 sts evenly across last row of rib (67 sts). Change to 3¼mm needles and k1 row. Next row: p17, MB, (p3, MB) 8 times, p17. Work 3 rows in st st. Repeat row 1; work 3 rows in st st. Row 9: p1, MB, (p3, MB) 16 times, p1. This sets your pattern of

bobbles. The vertical lines of bobbles should be repeated throughout, placing a complete horizontal line across the next and 2 following 48th rows. *At the same time*, inc 1 st at each end of every 15th row until you have 85 sts.

Shape sleeve top: cont bobble pattern, cast off 5 sts at beg of the next 2 rows, then dec 1 st at each end of every row until 63 sts remain. Dec 1 st at each end of every alt row until 31 sts remain. Cast off 4 sts at beg of the next 4 rows. Cast off remaining sts. Join one shoulder.

Neckband

Using a 2¾mm circular needle and with RS of work facing, pick up and knit 158 sts evenly around neck. K1, p1 rib for 2 rows. Cast off.

Making up

Join sleeves to body using a narrow backstitch. Join sleeve and side seams with a flat seam; join neck rib.

TARTAN TABBY KIDS KNIT

Materials
Melinda Coss mohair –
emerald: 150/175/200gm;
white, charcoal and
silver: less than 25gm of
each; oddments of black
and blue wool; tartan
ribbon: 0.5m.

Needles
One pair of 5mm and one
pair of 6mm needles.

Tension
Using 6mm needles and
measured over st st, 16
sts and 18 rows = 10cm
square.

Instructions are given in three sizes for this pattern featuring a smart tabby cat with a tartan bow. Worked using stocking stitch and the intarsia method (*see* Techniques, pages 9–10).

Front

Using 5mm needles and main colour, cast on 40/44/48 sts. Work in k2, p2 rib for 4cm, inc 14 sts evenly across last row of rib (54/58/62 sts).* Change to 6mm needles and work 4/6/8 rows in st st in main colour only. Begin working graph positioning as follows: k8/10/12 sts. Work first row of graph. K7/9/11 sts. This sets your position. Cont as set until graph is complete. Work 2/4/6 rows in main colour only.

Shape neck: work 21/22/24 sts. Cast off centre 14 sts. **Slip the first set of sts onto a stitch holder, work to end. Working on this last set of sts only, dec 1 st at neck edge on the next 6 rows. Work straight for 9 rows. Cast off remaining 15/16/18 sts.** Rep from ** to ** for other side of neck.

Back

Work as for front to *. Work in st st until back matches front to shoulder. Cast off.

Sleeves (2 alike)

Using 5mm needles, cast on 28 sts. K2, p2 rib for 4cm, inc 0/0/4 sts evenly across the last row of rib. Change to 6mm needles and cont in st st, using main colour only and inc 1 st at each end of every 4th row until you have 46/48/54 sts. Work without shaping for 2/2/3 rows. Cast off. Join one shoulder seam.

Neckband

Using 5mm needles, pick up 66/68/68 sts evenly around the neck. Work in k2, p2 rib for 20 rows. Cast off loosely. Slip stitch cast-off edge to pick-up edge, turning neckband inwards.

Making up

Join all seams using a flat seam. Embroider as indicated, using blue wool for the eyes. Tie ribbon into a bow. Sew into position where a cross is shown on the graph.

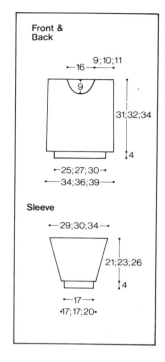

Incorporate this graph in the front of the Tartan Tabby jumper. Solid black lines show embroidery detail.

LION IN THE MOONLIGHT

A cotton bouclé, crew-necked, drop-sleeved jumper worked using the intarsia method (*see* Techniques, pages 9–10).

Materials
Melinda Coss cotton bouclé – white: 400gm; blue: 200gm; coffee, chestnut and yellow: 50gm; a few scraps of black.

Needles
One pair of 3½mm and one pair of 4mm needles.

Tension
Using 4mm needles and measured over st st, 18 sts and 24 rows = 10cm square.

N.B. Stitches
Loop stitch – on purl rows only: hold 3rd finger of left hand over yarn behind work, k1 (so that yarn forms loop around finger) but do not slip this stitch from needle; instead, transfer the stitch just worked back onto the left-hand needle and k2 through back loop (the stitch just knitted and the original stitch). Remove finger from loop ready for next stitch. (Make loop whenever 'X' appears on graph.)

Front
Using 3½mm needles and white, cast on 80 sts. K1, p1 rib for 7cm, inc 8 sts evenly along last row of rib (88 sts).★ Change to 4mm needles and, starting with a purl row, follow graph in st st to row 125. Work 38 sts, cast off centre 12 sts, work to end. Working on the last set of sts only, dec 1 st at neck edge on next 12 rows. Work 2 rows. Next row (WS): cast off 11 sts, p to end. Cast off remaining 15 sts. Rep neck shaping for other side of neck.

Back
Work as for front to ★. Cont in st st in white only until 89 rows have been worked. Change to blue and cont straight until back matches front to shoulder shaping. Cast off 11 sts at beg of the next 2 rows. Cast off 15 sts at beg of the following 2 rows. Cast off remaining 36 sts.

Sleeves
Using 3½mm needles and white, cast on 40 sts. Work in k1, p1 rib for 7cm. Change to 4mm needles and work in st st in white only, inc 1 st at each end of every 5th row. When work measures 39cm, change to blue and cont inc as set until you have 70 sts. Work without further shaping until sleeve measures 44cm from start. Cast off loosely. Join one shoulder seam.

Neckband
Using 3½mm needles and blue, pick up and knit 78 sts evenly around the neck. Work in k1, p1 rib for 8 rows, cast off loosely.

Embroidery
Add eyes, nose, mouth and whiskers (*see* diagram for instructions).

Making up
Join sleeve seams using narrow backstitch. Join neckband, sleeve and body seams with an invisible seam.

EMBROIDERY

Make yellow circle — Black — White

Black — Sand

Eyes   *Using 'D', bring needle up through back of work at the top of the eye. Make a circle and catch into place by making three small stitches as indicated. Change to white and, using large horizontal stitches, fill in the bottom of the eye. Change to black and using vertical stitches fill in the eyeball.*

Nose   *Using black, make a square by sewing four large stitches. Fill in with large vertical stitches. Bring needle up at bottom centre of nose and make one large downward stitch. For mouth, make one long horizontal stitch and catch in the middle with a small stitch as indicated.*

Whiskers   *Using 'B', cut two lengths of approx 10cm. Thread these separately across the back of the nose and knot securely into place. Pull the yarn to separate the fibres and trim as required.*

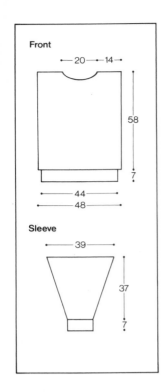

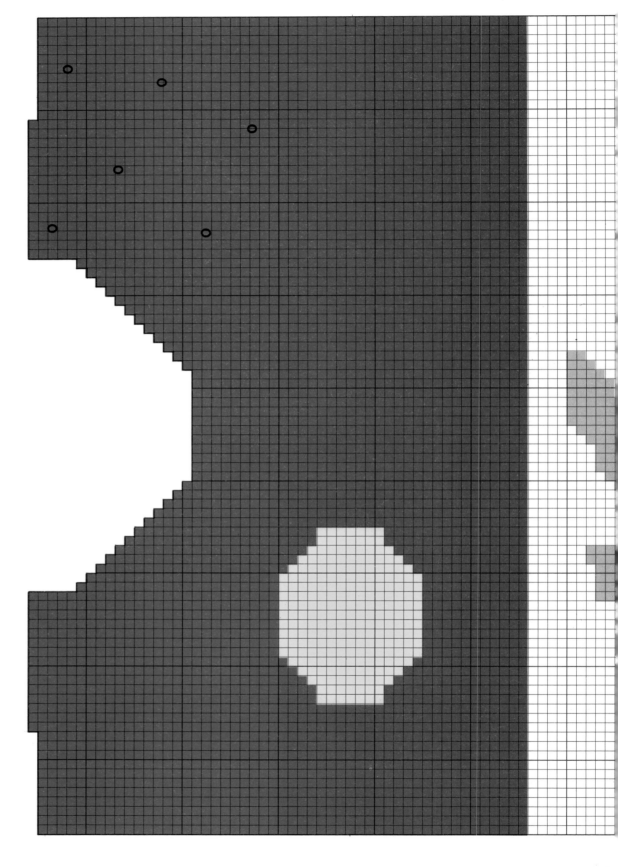

Graph for the front of the sweater. The graph has been reproduced horizontally but you should knit it vertically. The lion's mane is formed from loops of wool marked '×'. For embroidery instructions, see the diagram on page 82.

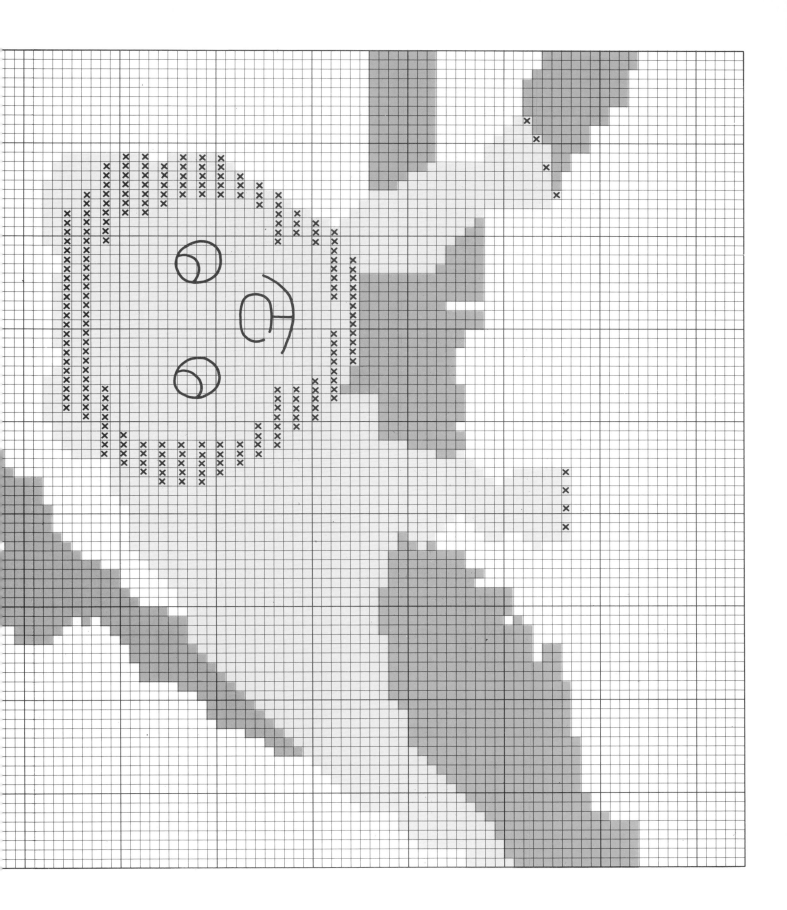

FLUFFY TORTOISESHELL KIDS KNIT

Materials
Melinda Coss mohair –
turquoise: 150/200/
250gm; black, cream,
chestnut, caramel,
chocolate and ginger: less
than 25gm of each. An
oddment of green.

Needles
One pair of 5mm and one
pair of 6mm needles.

Tension
Using 6mm needles and
measured over st st, 16
sts and 18 rows = 10cm
square. Ribs worked on
5mm needles.

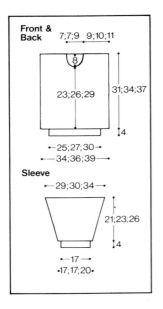

A warm, soft, fluffy jumper featuring
Tabitha cat. Instructions are given in three
sizes for children. The pattern is simple to
knit using mainly stocking stitch and the
intarsia method (*see* Techniques,
pages 9–10).

Front

Using 5mm needles and main colour, cast on 40/44/48 sts and work in k2, p2 rib for 4cm, inc 14 sts evenly across last row of rib. Change to 6mm needles★ and work 0/4/8 rows in st st in main colour. Begin working from graph, positioning as follows: k4/6/8 sts. Work first row of graph, k4/6/8 sts. This sets your position. Cont as set until graph is complete, then work 2/3/4 rows in main colour only.

Shape neck: work 21/22/24 sts. Cast off centre 14 sts. Slip the first set of sts on to a stitch holder, work to end. Working on the last set of sts only, dec 1 st at neck edge on the next 6 rows. Work straight for 9 rows. Cast off remaining 15/16/18 sts. Repeat for other side of neck.

Back

Work as for front to ★. Work in st st in main colour only for 57/63/67 rows. Cast off.

Sleeves (2 alike)

Using 5mm needles, cast on 28 sts. K2, p2 rib for 4cm, inc 0/0/4 sts evenly across the last row of rib. Change to 6mm needles and cont in st st, using main colour only and inc 1 st at each end of every 4th row until you have 46/48/54 sts. Work without shaping for 2/2/3 rows. Cast off. Join one shoulder seam.

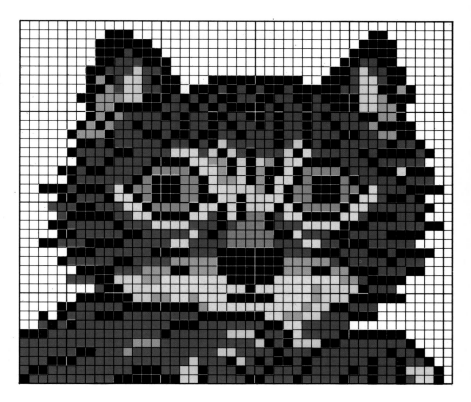

Incorporate the graph above in the front of the Tortoiseshell sweater.

Neckband

Using 5mm needles, pick up 66/68/68 sts evenly around the neck. Work in k2, p2 rib for 20 rows. Cast off loosely. Slip stitch cast-off edge to pick-up edge, turning neckband inwards.

Making up

Join all seams using a flat seam. Embroider as indicated.

EGG-COSIES

These three fun egg-cosies are knitted from the same graphs that are used for the brick-wall jacket illustrated on page 30 and are worked using the intarsia method (*see* Techniques, pages 8–9).

(Knitted in one piece)
Using 3¼mm needles and silver, cast on 44 sts. Work in k1, p1 rib for 6 rows, inc 6 sts evenly across last row of rib. Change to 4½mm needles and, starting with a knit row, work 4 rows in st st. Commence following selected graph, positioning as follows: k12, k25 from graph, k13. Cont with graph in this position until it is complete. Work 4 rows in main colour

only. Break off yarn and thread it back through the sts. Gather up tightly, oversew a couple of sts to secure. Turn cosy inside out and join side seam.

Tassel

Wind main colour yarn around your left hand 10 times. Slip the loops off your hand and fold loops in half. Wind wool tightly around the bottom of the yarn and oversew to secure. Trim ends of tassels. Sew tassel to top of cosy through bottom knot.

Materials

Melinda Coss DK – silver: 50gm; oddments of camel, ginger, black, white, cream and blue.

Needles

One pair of 3¼mm and one pair of 4½mm needles.

Tension

Using 4½mm needles and measured over st st, 26 sts and 30 rows = 10cm square. Welts worked on 3¼mm needles.

Tea-cosy graphs are on pages 89/90.

CAT TEA-COSY

Made in double-knitting wool, this cat tea-cosy is worked entirely in stocking stitch using the intarsia method (*see* Techniques, pages 9–10).

Front

Using beige and 4½mm needles, cast on 69 sts. Begin following graph in st st, inc 1 st at each end of the first 2 alt rows. Inc 1 st at the beg of the next row and at the end of the following row. Work shapings as indicated on the graph until row 60 is complete.

Shape ears: cont to follow the graph, k7, turn, p2 tog, p to end. Cast off remaining 6 sts. Rejoin yarn at inner ear. K2 tog, k to end. Next row: p9, turn, cast off 9 sts, rejoin yarn to inner ear. Cast off 3 sts, p to end. Next row: cast off 2 sts, k to end. Turn, cast off remaining sts.

Back

Work as for front, but commence with a purl row – i.e., read rows from right to left as purl and from left to right as knit. Follow the appropriate graph.

Materials
Melinda Coss DK wool – chocolate, ginger, beige, white, gold, pink, black and silver: less than 50gm of each; terylene wadding: 0.5m.

Needles
One pair of 4½mm needles.

Tension
Using 4½mm needles and measured over st st, 28 rows and 22 sts = 10cm square.

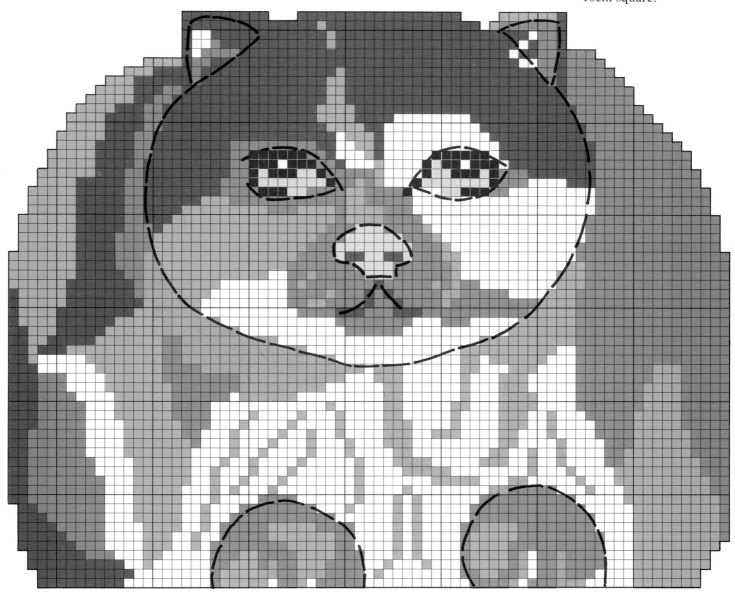

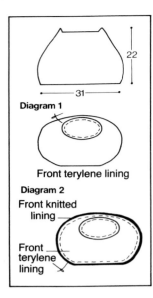

Diagram 1

Front terylene lining

Diagram 2

Front knitted lining

Front terylene lining

Front lining

Using silver, cast on 65 sts and work in st st, using silver only and following graph shapings for front until row 56 is complete. Cast off.

Back lining

Work as for front lining, but commence with a purl row.

Making up

Press both pieces using a damp cloth. Lay the pieces out on the terylene wadding and cut two pieces of wadding to match the front and back. Cut a circle of wadding the size of the cat's head and tack this to the front wadding shape as shown in diagram 1. Set these aside.

Take the front and back knitted lining pieces and sew these together (WS facing), leaving the bottom edge open. Tack the two pieces of terylene lining on to the knitted lining (diagram 2).

Place cat front and back RS facing and join together. Turn inside out. Place inner lining into position and stitch neatly around the bottom edge. Embroider as shown on the graph, carrying thread through the three thicknesses of knitting and wadding to create a quilted effect.

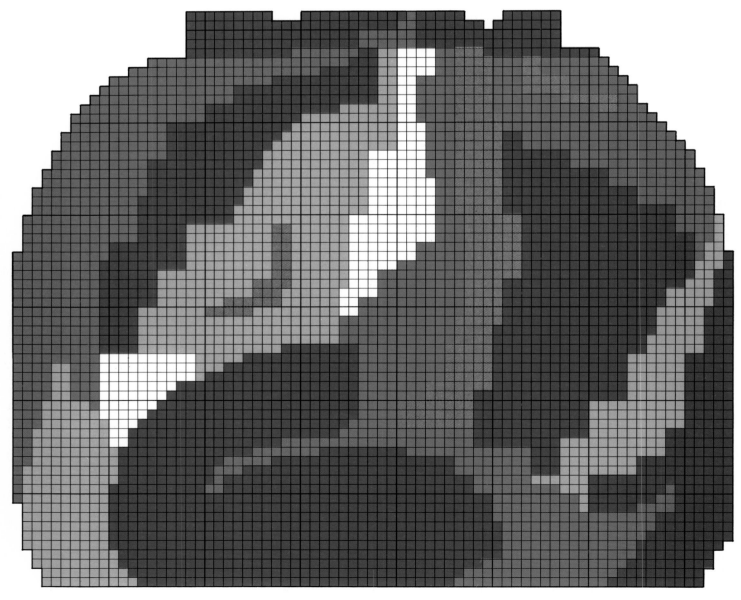

FLUFFY KITTEN TOY

This fluffy mohair kitten is simple to knit and makes a wonderful pet to play with.

Stitches

Garter stitch throughout (knit every row).

Body and legs

Starting with the rear legs and using 5mm needles, cast on 20 sts and k 24 rows. Leave these sts on a spare needle. Work another leg the same, then knit across both sets of sts to join them together. Next row: *k13, knit twice into each of the next 14 sts, k13. K 12 rows straight. Next row: k13, (k2 tog) 14 times. K13.* K 31 rows, rep from * to * once more. K 1 row. Next row: k 20, turn, leave remaining sts on a spare needle. K 20 rows straight on these 20 sts. Cast off. Rejoin yarn to remaining 20 sts. K 20 rows, cast off.

Pads (Make 4)

Cast on 3 sts, k 1 row, inc 1 st at each end of next row, rep the last 2 rows twice more. K 1 row, dec 1 st at each end of next row. Repeat last 2 rows until 3 sts remain. Cast off.

Head

Cast on 18 sts. K 10 rows. Next row: k3. Knit twice into each of the next 13 sts. K2. K 11 rows. Next row: k3, (k2 tog) 13 times, k2. K 56 rows. Cast off.

Tail

Cast on 22 sts. K 14 rows, dec 1 st at each end of the next row and every following 5th row until 14 sts remain. Dec at each end of every following 10th row until 8 sts remain, then dec at each end of every alt row to the remaining 4 sts. Cast off.

Gusset

Starting at the tail end, cast on 4 sts. K 2 rows. Inc 1 st at each end of the next row and the 8 following 3rd rows. Dec 1 st at each end of the following 3rd row and the 8 following 4th rows. K 3 rows. Cast off.

Making up

Fold each leg in half lengthways and join seams using a flat seam. Stitch pads to bottom of legs. Stitch gusset into position, leaving a small opening at the top, and stuff

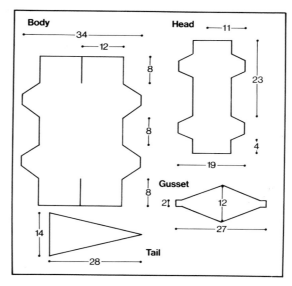

Materials
Melinda Coss mohair – white or ginger: 75gm. One pair of green glass cat's eyes ¾cm wide; 61cm of ribbon.

Needles
One pair of 5mm needles.

Tension
Using 5mm needles and measured over garter st, 16 sts and 24 rows = 10cm square.

firmly. Fold head in half and, using backstitch, stitch diagonally across corners to make ears (see diagram). Place glass eyes in position and embroider nose and mouth using satin stitch. Join side seams of head, leaving opening at the bottom, and stuff firmly, using extra stuffing for cheeks. Attach head to body over front legs by over-sewing. Fold tail in half lengthways and join edges together. Oversew tail into position above back legs.

Make whiskers: thread a double length of mohair, approx 12cm long, through face to come out either side of nose. Knot each side to secure position. Tie ribbon around neck.

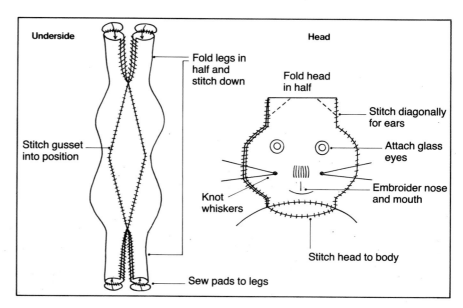

CAT CUSHION

This cat cushion is worked in double-knitting wool and angora and is knitted entirely in stocking stitch using the intarsia method (*see* Techniques, pages 9–10).

Materials
Melinda Coss DK wool – turquoise: 100gm; purple: 100gm; Melinda Coss angora – black, grey and white: less than 25gm of each; an oddment of yellow wool. A cushion pad approx 36cm square; a zip approx 32cm.

Needles
One pair of 4½mm needles.

Tension
Using 4½mm needles and measured over st st, 28 rows and 22 sts = 10cm square.

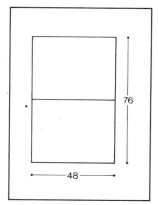

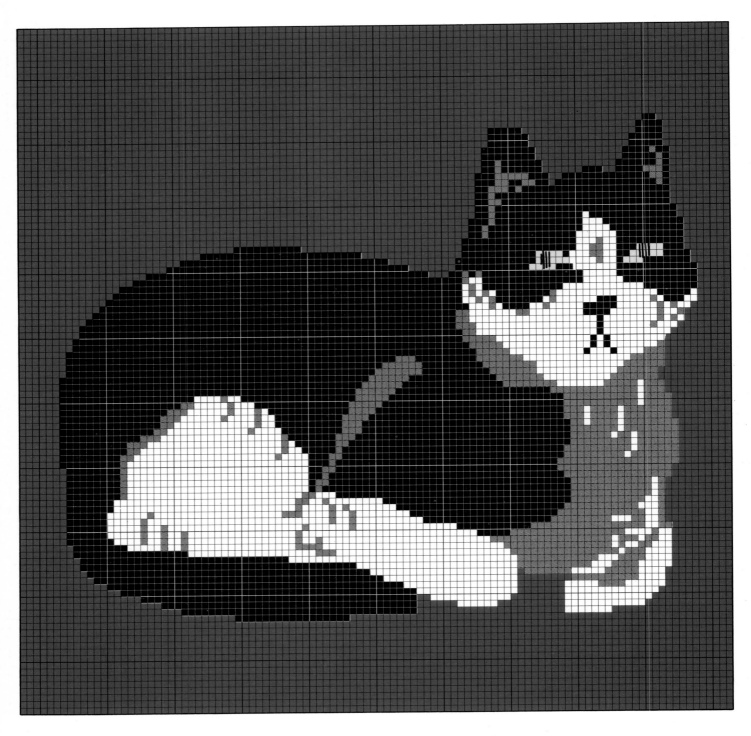

The graph above is the design for the front of the cat cushion.

The blank graph opposite is for you to design your own cat motif.

(Knitted in one piece)
Using purple and 4½mm needles, cast on 106 sts. Work graph entirely in st st until complete. Change to turquoise and work a further 106 rows in this colour only. Cast off.

Making up
Fold in half with RS facing. Join side seams using a narrow backstitch. Sew zip into position across bottom of cushion-cover. Embroider pupils of eyes using satin stitch.